University of Illinois
Urbana-Champaign

Written by Bridget Sharkey

Edited by Kelly Carey and Kimberly Moore

Layout by Jon Skindzier

*Additional contributions by Omid Gohari,
Christina Koshzow, Chris Mason, Joey Rahimi,
and Luke Skurman*

ISBN # 1-4274-0171-3
ISSN # 1552-1338
© Copyright 2006 College Prowler
All Rights Reserved
Printed in the U.S.A.
www.collegeprowler.com

Last updated 5/16/06

Special Thanks To: Babs Carryer, Andy Hannah, LaunchCyte, Tim O'Brien, Bob Sehlinger, Thomas Emerson, Andrew Skurman, Barbara Skurman, Bert Mann, Dave Lehman, Daniel Fayock, Chris Babyak, The Donald H. Jones Center for Entrepreneurship, Terry Slease, Jerry McGinnis, Bill Ecenberger, Idie McGinty, Kyle Russell, Jacque Zaremba, Larry Winderbaum, Roland Allen, Jon Reider, Team Evankovich, Lauren Varacalli, Abu Noaman, Mark Exler, Daniel Steinmeyer, Jared Cohon, Gabriela Oates, David Koegler, Glen Meakem, and the University of Illinois Bounce-Back Team.

College Prowler®
5001 Baum Blvd.
Suite 750
Pittsburgh, PA 15213

Phone: 1-800-229-4675
Fax: 1-800-772-4972
E-Mail: info@collegeprowler.com
Web Site: www.collegeprowler.com

Welcome to

During the writing of College Prowler's guidebooks, we felt it was critical that our content was unbiased and unaffiliated with any college or university. We think it's important that our readers get honest information and a realistic impression of the student opinions on any campus—that's why if any aspect of a particular school is terrible, we (unlike a campus brochure) intend to publish it. While we do keep an eye out for the occasional extremist—the cheerleader or the cynic—we take pride in letting the students tell it like it is. We strive to create a book that's as representative as possible of each particular campus. Our books cover both the good and the bad, and whether the survey responses point to recurring trends or a variation in opinion, these sentiments are directly and proportionally expressed through our guides.

College Prowler guidebooks are in the hands of students throughout the entire process of their creation. Because you can't make student-written guides without the students, we have students at each campus who help write, randomly survey their peers, edit, layout, and perform accuracy checks on every book that we publish. From the very beginning, student writers gather the most up-to-date stats, facts, and inside information on their colleges. They fill each section with student quotes and summarize the findings in editorial reviews. In addition, each school receives a collection of letter grades (A through F) that reflect student opinion and help to represent contentment, prominence, or satisfaction for each of our 20 specific categories. Just as in grade school, the higher the mark the more content, more prominent, or more satisfied the students are with the particular category.

Once a book is written, additional students serve as editors and check for accuracy even more extensively. Our bounce-back team—a group of randomly selected students who have no involvement with the project—are asked to read over the material in order to help ensure that the book accurately expresses every aspect of the university and its students. This same process is applied to the 200-plus schools College Prowler currently covers. Each book is the result of endless student contributions, hundreds of pages of research and writing, and countless hours of hard work. All of this has led to the creation of a student information network that stretches across the nation to every school that we cover. It's no easy accomplishment, but it's the reason that our guides are such a great resource.

When reading our books and looking at our grades, keep in mind that every college is different and that the students who make up each school are not uniform—as a result, it is important to assess schools on a case-by-case basis. Because it's impossible to summarize an entire school with a single number or description, each book provides a dialogue, not a decision, that's made up of 20 different topics and hundreds of student quotes. In the end, we hope that this guide will serve as a valuable tool in your college selection process. Enjoy!

OMID GOHARI ◯ CHRISTINA KOSHZOW ◯ CHRIS MASON ◯ JOEY RAHIMI ◯ LUKE SKURMAN ◯
The College Prowler Team

Table of Contents

Introduction from the Author

When you grow up in Illinois, you hear about the University of Illinois from about the time you can crawl. If you don't have family there, your friends generally do, or maybe your grade school teacher graduated from there. U of I is a familiar place to most Illinois high school students, both in personal ties and in distance. Located in Central Illinois, the University is almost equidistant from Southern Illinois as Northern Illinois, meaning that whether you grew up near St. Louis or near Chicago, it is only a couple of hours away.

Not only is U of I close to home for Illinois natives, it also offers comfortable and welcoming surroundings. While some people imagine themselves as Felicity, off to tackle the dangers of New York City alone, the reality is that most of us U of I students come from rural neighborhoods. Most of the students grew up next to cornfields and barns, even if those fields were only an hour away from the Arch or the Sears Tower. U of I has all the people and the excitement that a big city would have, minus the pollution and crime. In fact, the only pollution in the air comes from the cow barns north of campus. Although students sometimes complain about living in the middle of cornfields, they are still very comfortable and relaxed in their surroundings. Even if they may choose to tackle big city living after graduation, few regret having spent their college years on a safe yet exciting campus.

Of course, academics are the main reason for the University's success. It's engineering and business schools rival colleges across the nation, and their agriculture department is understandably very popular. A degree from the University of Illinois holds both prestige and promise, which is something I realized from the pleased responses people make when they hear what college I attend. A respected degree at a public tuition cost is not easily found, but for those of us in the state, it is only a short drive away.

The University of Illinois is certainly not right for everyone, however. Maybe you want to go to a small school. Maybe you want to go to school in an urban metropolis. Maybe you are looking for an art school and not a state school. Whatever the case, this guidebook is intended to show you, as honestly as possible, the pros and cons of this university.

Bridget Sharkey, Author
University of Illinois

By the Numbers

General Information

University of Illinois
601 E. John Street
Champaign, IL 61820

Control:
Public

Academic Calendar:
Semester

Religious Affiliation:
None

Founded:
1867

Web Site:
www.uiuc.edu

Main Phone:
(217) 333-0824

Admissions Phone:
(217) 333-0302

Student Body

**Full-Time
Undergraduates:**
28,686

**Part-Time
Undergraduates:**
986

**Total Male
Undergraduates:**
15,601

**Total Female
Undergraduates:**
14,031

Admissions

Overall Acceptance Rate:
68%

Total Applicants:
21,914

Total Acceptances:
14,921

Freshman Enrollment:
7,284

Early Decision Available?
Yes

Early Action Available?
No

Regular Decision Deadline:
January 1

Regular Decision Notification:
April 1

Must-Reply-By Date:
May 1

Yield (Percent of admitted students who actually enroll):
49%

Applicants Placed on Waiting List:
3,032

Applicants Accepted from Waiting List:
1,506

Students Enrolled from Waiting List:
1,186

Transfer Applications Received:
2,630

Transfer Applications Accepted:
1,409

Transfer Student Yield:
77%

Common Application Accepted?
No

Supplemental Forms?
Yes

Admissions E-Mail:
undergraduate@admissions.
uiuc.edu

Admissions Web Site:
www.oar.uiuc.edu

SAT I or ACT Required?
Either

First-Year Students Submitting SAT Scores:
87%

SAT I Range (25th–75th Percentile):
1180–1400

SAT I Verbal Range (25th–75th Percentile):
560–670

SAT I Math Range (25th–75th Percentile):
620–730

Retention Rate:
92%

Application Fee:
$40

**Top 10% of
High School Class:**
50%

Financial Information

In-State Tuition:
$8,624

Out-Of-State Tuition:
$22,710

Room and Board:
$6,848

Books and Supplies:
$950

**Average Need-Based
Financial Aid Package
(including loans, work-study,
grants, and other sources):**
$8,918

**Students Who
Applied for Financial Aid:**
61%

Students Who Received Aid:
44%

Financial Aid Forms Deadline:
March 15

Financial Aid Phone:
(217) 333-0100

Financial Aid Web Site:
www.ofsa.uiuc.edu

Academics

The Lowdown On...
Academics

Degrees Awarded:
Bachelor
Master
Doctorate
First Professional

Most Popular Majors:
17% Business
14% Engineering
10% Social Sciences
 9% English
 7% Economics

Undergraduate Schools:
College of Agricultural, Consumer, and Environmental Sciences

College of Applied Life Studies

College of Business

College of Communications

College of Education

College of Engineering

College of Fine and Applied Arts

College of Law

College of Liberal Arts and Sciences

➡

(Undergraduate Schools, continued)

College of Medicine at Urbana-Champaign

College of Veterinary Medicine

Graduate College

Graduate School of Library and Information Science

Institute of Aviation

Institute of Labor and Industrial Relations

Sargent College of Health and Rehabilitation Sciences

School of Social Work

University Professors Program

Full-Time Faculty:

2,158

Faculty with Terminal Degree:

85%

Student-to-Faculty Ratio:

14:1

Average Course Load:

Five

Graduation Rates:

Four-Year: 58%

Five-Year: 78%

Six-Year: 80%

AP Test Score Requirements

Possible credit for scores of 4 or 5

Special Degree Options

Dual-Degree Programs, English and Rhetoric, Marital and Family Services

Sample Academic Clubs

Academic Buzzer Team, Africa-in-Academics, Students Association, DesignBuildFly, Hoof and Horn

Best Places to Study

Main or Undergrad Library, Illini Union, Quad

Did You Know?

U of I offers Discovery Courses for all freshmen. These classes are small and geared towards first-year students. Instead of being overwhelmed by a huge lecture class in their freshman year, students can participate in class and have one-on-one discussions with the teacher.

The Writers' Workshop offers free writing help for all students. You can walk in with a rough draft and walk out with a polished paper, free of grammatical errors and writing goofs.

U of I has Learning Communities. These are groups of 18 freshmen that take 3 classes together. One of the classes is a meeting, a time in which the freshmen discuss issues pertinent to first-year students. Participating in a learning community is a great way to make friends and become acclimated to surroundings. In a 500-person lecture, it's good to recognize a familiar face, not to mention 17 familiar faces.

U of I boasts the third largest academic library in North America, topped only by Yale and Harvard. This makes it the largest public university library in existence.

Vodafone, one of the largest mobile telecommunications network companies in the world, recently donated a $3.3 million grant to the College of Engineering, naming it one of the best engineering programs in the country.

Students Speak Out On...
Academics

"All of my classes have been good, but my favorite was Sociology 225. The teachers seem well-informed."

Q "The geography department has **good classes**. I am just a freshman, but so far, classes are good."

Q "**I never thought any of my classes were too hard**, so far, anyhow. I never had a problem with any of the teachers or TAs."

Q "I've never had a problem with teachers or classes. All have been **good experiences**."

Q "The classes are not bad, but I had a problem with a teacher once. It was a political science class, and I think **the teacher was racist in a way**."

Q "The faculty is pretty good. I am in the math department, so **there is a social intimidation factor**—only in the math department, though. I don't know why they are like that."

Q "**I enjoyed my classes and my teachers**. Some more than others of course, but overall everything is good."

Q "I have liked almost all of my classes. The teachers have **always been available at office hours**, and they are generally accessible. I have no complaints."

Q "Teachers are generally well-meaning. Some are more concerned with their research than with their teaching. Classes are usually **at least somewhat interesting** depending on the class and the teacher. Classes are interesting if you make them interesting."

Q "**The teachers vary greatly**, but they are all involved with their material and are knowledgeable about the content of their course. This makes the courses interesting because you realize how much you can learn from them."

Q "It is amazing to see how all of your classes begin to tie together and how **you can connect the ideas** and apply them to yourself and society."

Q "Truthfully, **it can be a bit of a gamble**. Usually you have good teachers. Then you get an awesome one. Then you get one you absolutely hate. It is all relative."

Q "It is **the third-best engineering school** in the country."

Q "**Pretty good**. Some TAs are foreign, and it is not easy to understand them, but that occurs mainly in the math and science departments."

Q "**It's different than high school**—you have to do 70 percent of the teaching to yourself by reading a lot. You can always get help, whether you go to office hours or get a tutor."

Q "Many professors are approachable, **research opportunities are available**, and once beyond the first year or so, a student will have the opportunity to directly interact with the professor in a classroom setting."

Q "If you need assistance, **teachers strongly encourage you to see them**. They find a way to get you into their office, to work with you one-on-one, and to answer any questions you might have."

Q "Most instructors set reasonable guidelines and do well at handling each individual on a personal basis. **The discussions are small, and office hours are flexible**, so it's easy to get one-on-one time."

Q "There are so many instructors that the styles and personalities of each vary widely. The TAs are relaxed and liberal, especially about writing and research methods. Some of them are accepting of the Internet as primary sources whereas the professors stress going to the library and going through printed sources. We have the world's foremost war historian—he has **written several books on the art of war**—teaching one of our most challenging history courses. Many of the English, philosophy, and history professors show more personality and encourage exploration of ideas more. The engineering, math, and chemistry/biology professors are rigid and assign a lot of work. Most instructors set reasonable guidelines and do well at handling each student on a personal basis. The discussions are small and office hours are flexible. Although, one out of every eight instructors will most likely be an asshole; it's like some type of university bylaw."

Q "The professors and teaching assistants at UIUC are very accessible to students. Regular office hours, during which **students can meet with the instructor**, are required. The phone number and office location of professors and teaching assistants are available to students so that meetings can be set up outside of office hours. If a student finds a problem with a teaching assistant or professor, she or he can always contact that person's superior to resolve the matter."

Q "In almost every field, the University of Illinois boasts prominent professors that are internationally known. Unfortunately, due to the class size, in the first year or two, a student will not experience direct work under a professor, but with a teaching assistant, typically a graduate student. **Many professors are approachable**, research opportunities are available, and eventually, a student will have the opportunity to directly interact with the professor in a classroom setting."

Q "The staff and faculty at the U of I are said to be among the most scholarly in the nation according to its Web site. And when you're at a competitive university like this one, this is what one might expect. I have encountered the best and the worst of them. The best are those individuals that care about your progress. They know that, for example, you are not an expert in English literature; **you are here to learn and are open to constructive criticism**. If you need assistance, they strongly encourage you to see them."

Q "There are good teachers, and there are bad teachers. The pattern that can be seen in the bad teachers is their nonchalant attitude when you come in for office hours or when they are **too critical of your work** and do not acknowledge progress. Some do not care to improve their teaching strategies even if they have been told to do so."

Q "If you need assistance, **teachers strongly encourage you to see them**. They find a way to get you into their office, to work with you one-on-one, and to answer any questions you might have."

The College Prowler Take On...
Academics

The University's business and agricultural programs are world-renowned and very popular. However, the liberal arts and sciences departments are not as prestigious. Students often complain about the state of the English Building compared to the state of the engineering building, claming that arts majors are passed over in favor of other majors. However, U of I still has a great drama and writing department, and it has recently added a creative writing master's degree. Efforts are being made to reach out to other interests, but the bulk of this school is still the engineering department. If that's your interest, U of I is definitely a competitive choice.

Many professors are dedicated to teaching and reaching out to their students. Most make themselves available, and a few have even been known to give out their home phone number. Still, it can be hard to get acclimated to a school of 28,000, which is why the University implemented discussion groups to accompany big lectures. Unfortunately, these discussion groups are generally led by a TA repeating the week's points in a monotone voice. If you want help outside of class, the best bet is office hours or online notes. Most big classes, such as general education classes, have a Web site with online notes and PowerPoint presentations, so you never miss anything, even if you skip a class or can't keep up with the teacher's notes. Of course, every university has terrible teachers, but the faculty is generally well-informed and caring, and every once in a while, you meet a really great teacher who inspires you.

B

The College Prowler® Grade on
Academics: B

A high Academics grade generally indicates that professors are knowledgeable, accessible, and genuinely interested in their students' welfare. Other determining factors include class size, how well professors communicate, and whether or not classes are engaging.

Local Atmosphere

The Lowdown On...
Local Atmosphere

Region:
Midwest

City, State:
Urbana-Champaign, IL

Setting:
Small, rural twin cities

Distance from Chicago:
2.5 hours

Distance from St. Louis:
2.5 hours

Points of Interest:
Allerton Park
The Alma Mater
The Armory
Foellinger Auditorium
Krannert Art Museum
Morrow Plots
Spurlock Museum

→

Closest Movie Theaters:

Beverly Cinemas
910 Meijer Drive, Champaign
(217) 359-5687

Goodrich Savoy 16 Theater
232 Burwash Avenue, Savoy
(217) 355-9475

New Art Theater
126 West Church Street
(217) 351-7368

Closest Shopping Malls:

Farmer's Market
Lincoln Square Mall
Market Place Mall

Major Sports Teams:

Chicago Bears (football)
Chicago Blackhawks (hockey)
Chicago Bulls (basketball)
Chicago Cubs (baseball)
Chicago White Sox (baseball)
St. Louis Cardinals (baseball)
St. Louis Rams (football)
St. Louis Blues (hockey)

Did You Know?

5 Fun Facts about Champaign:

- Urbana-Champaign was named one of the world's **"10 Hot New Tech Cities"** by *Newsweek*.
- **Famous alumnus Hugh Hefner** allegedly donated every issue of *Playboy* to the University.
- **The auditorium of Foellinger** was used in the graduation scene of the Brendan Fraser movie *With Honors*.
- **Special cows at South Farms** have holes cut into their bellies, which allows vet students to take samples from their insides while the cows are still living.
- **The English Building was once a dormitory**, and a pool was originally in the present sunken lounge. Legend has it that a girl from that old dormitory still haunts the English Building halls, and many students say strange occurrences have happened to them late at night in the computer lab.

➡

Famous People from Champaign:

Hugh Hefner (founder of *Playboy*); Andy Richter (actor/comedian); Roger Ebert (film critic); Ken Holtzman (Cubs pitcher); Phil Baker (CEO, Proctor and Gamble); Ken Dilger (Super Bowl champ, Tampa Bay Buccaneers tight end); Harold "Red" Grange (Chicago Bears Hall of Fame running back); James Cantalupo (president of McDonald's International); Dr. Harold Osborn (1924 Olympic gold medalist, track and field); Jerry Hadley (Opera Singer); Robert Falls (Tony Award winner); and Michael Colgrass and George Crumb (Pulitzer Prize winners and composers).

Local Slang:

Pop – What people from Northern Illinois call soda

Brewski – Chicago slang for beer

Toasted Ravioli – Breaded pasta from St. Louis/Southwestern Illinois

Chi-Town – Another name for Chicago

Windy City – Yet another name for Chicago

Aggie – Someone majoring in Agriculture

Butt – Adjective for ugly

City Web Sites

www.uiuc.edu/community

www.cucvb.org

www.city.urbana.il.us

Students Speak Out On...
Local Atmosphere

{ **"The atmosphere is just campus life, really. The recreational areas are the places where everyone is. There isn't much interaction with other colleges in the area."**

Q "There is something for everyone here. It's a varied atmosphere. **Stuff is always going on**."

Q "**There is a lot to do here**. You can go to the gym and work out or play games. Yeah, there are bars and other stuff, too, but that's not everything."

Q "The campus sponsors **several events almost every weekend**. Of course, there are always parties and other stuff, too."

Q "There is a lot to do, but it usually involves parties and bars. **Not much else goes on here**."

Q "There is **a lot to do here**, but not if you don't look for it. If you sit at home and do nothing, you will think there is nothing to do. You have to get out there."

Q "The atmosphere—well, **Green Street is always happening**. Always stuff to do there."

Q "The atmosphere is nice—that of a small, Midwestern city. The people are nice, and the town is cozy. It is large enough to have plenty to do without being too big and overwhelming. **There is a community college in town** and a few other colleges within an hour's drive away."

Q "You can chill at a variety of parks, the Krannert Art Museum, or go to any school sporting event like football or baseball, or maybe a play at the Krannert Center for the Performing Arts. Of course, the Custard Cup also has **the most famous ice cream in town**."

Q "For a state school, the University of Illinois is in an awkward spot. **A little more than two hours from Chicago and three from St. Louis,** the atmosphere of Urbana-Champaign is completely dictated by the events of the University. Aside from a small community college, there are no other universities present. However, other universities, such as Illinois State University and Illinois-Wesleyan are a little more than an hour away."

Q "The overall atmosphere in Urbana-Champaign is friendly and warm. But then again, **it is what you make of it**. Some people may think otherwise, but in my case, I was able to meet a lot of people on the first day because I was open and friendly. One thing that older U of I students and staff stress is to be open and get yourself out there if you want to meet people."

Q "One thing that I recommend is going to events that are sponsored by the Illini Union Board, or artistic or cultural events (fashion shows, film festivals, cultural taste exhibits, dance workshops). Also popular are free or affordable plays and concerts (including University organizations like Black Choir or outside bands like Dave Matthews). A lot of these things are affordable and sometimes even free; they know that college students are working on tight budgets. **Greek step shows are also really popular** (regular step shows are nice, but the Greek ones are said to be the best and are generally held toward the end of the year)."

Q "Parkland Community College is located in Champaign, and many U of I students take summer or online courses there to supplement their primary curricula or to fulfill general education requirements. Also, the historical Virginia Theater is located in Champagne, where U of I alum Roger Ebert holds his **annual Overlooked Film Festival**. The theater also plays classic or popular films that are well attended by the academic, student, and local communities."

Q "The best place to study or hang out has got to be the Illini Union—it has everything from restaurants to coffee shops to rest areas to arcade/game rooms. Between classes, students gather there to talk or to promote shows and different events. On hot days, there is air-conditioning! Coffee houses such as Moonstruck are also **mellow places to chill or to study**."

Q "The University is very isolated from the town of Champaign itself. The rest of the city is **impoverished for the most part**. Most students refer to the residents as townies."

Q "There are **tons of things to do in the city**, but you definitely have to know where you are going and what the crowd will be like."

Q "Urbana-Champaign combines the small-town country feel with the city atmosphere. It is an academic community, but walk, bike, or drive a few blocks into Urbana or Champaign, and **you'll enjoy the huge country homes set far back from the street**, the stretches of farmland, and tractors driving down the roads."

The College Prowler Take On...
Local Atmosphere

Urbana-Champaign is mostly farmland, except for the University, which is located in the middle of prairieland, bounded by farms and fields. The campus rises out of the middle of the twin citie,s and even with its popular main road, Green Street, the city is not at all an urban center. U of I has truly kept the small-town feel as much as possible. It is not a fast-paced city attempting to build the tallest skyscrapers, but rather a small town seeking to keep its rural roots. An example of this is the undergrad library, exactly the opposite of a skyscraper. The University decided to build it underground so that the shade from the building would not negatively affect the nearby research field, the Morrow Plots.

This does not mean that U of I is boring all of the time. It's a huge university with events and parties going on, but students say that you have to get out there and find out about them. Among the most popular happenings are Greek step shows, school sports games, and artsy events which are campus- or locally-sponsored. Some students feel that U of I can be dull after a while, yet in contrast, others say that the atmosphere is still warm and friendly. Some students do say that there are not many alternatives to the bar and club scene. Maybe this is why so many people go home on the weekends, choosing to visit friends and family rather than spend another weekend at the same old bar. Consider yourself warned: U of I is certainly not in the hick town some claim it is—except for the constant smell of manure—but it can become very dull.

B-

The College Prowler® Grade on

Local
Atmosphere: B-

A high Local Atmosphere grade indicates that the area surrounding campus is safe and scenic. Other factors include nearby attractions, proximity to other schools, and the town's attitude toward students.

Safety & Security

The Lowdown On...
Safety & Security

Number of University of Illinois Police:
55 sworn officers and 21 civilian security staff

Illinois Police Phone:
911
9-911 (campus phone)
(217) 333-1216
(non-emergencies)

Safety Services:
Blue emergency phones
SafeRides
Student Patrol Walking Escorts
Rape Aggression Defense System (RAD)

Health Services:
Basic medical care
Counseling services
Dial-A-Nurse Hotline (24/7)
Flu clinic
HIV/STD testing
On-site pharmaceuticals
Women's care

→

Health Center Office Hours:

Monday–Friday 8 a.m.–
5:30 p.m., Saturday 8 a.m.–
4:30 p.m., closed on Sunday

Did You Know?

The **Dial-A-Nurse hotline** is open all day, every day. You can call this number for assistance with a simple cold or even for suspected alcohol poisoning. The people who work there are comforting and give great advice, just what you need when you have a health problem and the clinic is closed.

Students Speak Out On...
Safety & Security

> "Safety services are really good here. There are late bus services and SafeRides. There are options if you choose to utilize them."

Q "**I always feel safe here**. I never had anything happen to me personally or heard about anything. Just don't walk alone at night; that's what everyone says."

Q "It is pretty safe. There are **always lights and emergency towers**. There are rides you can call, and they hand out whistles to all the girls."

Q "I never had a problem with security. I have **never heard about anything bad happening** to people I know."

Q "The way the school handles safety here is satisfactory. U of I takes steps to **promote safety**, I think."

Q "I have **always felt safe**. I think everyone does."

Q "I don't feel my life is in danger. But **I don't walk alone at night**. And I look over my shoulder."

Q "**The safety warnings are there**. You just have to take them."

Q "It is safe for the most part. Problems tend to arise as a result of **people not making smart decisions** (i.e. walking home alone at night)."

Q "Security and safety is **only as a big of an issue as one makes it** on campus. If one takes careful steps to avoid potentially dangerous situations, security will not be an issue."

Q "Though some people are worried about security on campus, the Quad and main campus grounds are really quite safe. Plus, there are groups of campus security who walk the Quad and campus to keep things safe. There are also **several emergency booths** if anything should happen."

Q "If one follows the advice from the safety classes the University requires every new student to take, such as never walking at night alone or always making sure one knows where a drink came from, **most problems can be avoided**."

Q "Since U of I is such a large university, security is pretty much top-notch. **They keep transportation running constantly**, especially at night and on weekends. When the buses do stop (on special holidays or during road construction), there are services such as SafeRides that will get you where you need to go day or night for free."

Q "Orientation really prepares students to deal with campus safety. **Every female is issued a rape whistle**. We have a workshop called C.A.R.E., which is mandatory by the end of your first semester, and it is very informative in dealing with issues of date rape but approaches it in an open-minded forum."

Q "The chancellor is constantly sending out mass e-mails to remind students to be safe and never to travel alone at night. **The police are on top of everything**, so much so that you can barely sneeze without causing an alarm, but it keeps the campus secure."

Q "Don't put yourself in bad situations, especially those involving alcohol and drugs. **Knowing your limits and setting boundaries** is the best way to stay safe."

Q "The dorms are secure after 7 p.m. so that **only persons with keys can be admitted to the general lobby** area. Floors are always locked in order to prevent unauthorized or dangerous people from wandering around. There is an enforced rule in the dorms that prohibits residents' guests from walking around unescorted."

The College Prowler Take On...
Safety & Security

U of I is always looking for better ways to protect its students. There are blue emergency phones scattered all over campus, and even if they are used as unofficial cigarette bins, they are there should you ever need them. Officers are present on campus, whether they are patrolling the bars at night, or monitoring speed limits in the daytime. SafeRides are also a valuable source. They operate from 9 p.m. to 6 a.m. and will drive University students to their dorm or apartment at no charge. So whether you are out late at the library or too drunk to drive home, SafeRides can be depended on. All the residence halls require either an outside key or an I-card after dark, so few non-students can slip in. Students know that the University is serious about their well-being, and they appreciate the security of the campus.

Emergency phones and SafeRides can only go so far. That is why the University tries to educate its students on the dangers that exist and the precautions that students should take. Whether it is a sign in the library reminding you not to leave your bag alone, or a workshop educating people on the dangers of rape drugs, U of I wants everyone to be in the know. Mass e-mails are sent out to all the students if there is increase in theft or assault crimes so that students can be especially careful when they travel the campus. All the resources are there, and if you choose to utilize them, your time at U of I should be very safe and uneventful.

B+

The College Prowler® Grade on

Safety & Security: B+

A high grade in Safety & Security means that students generally feel safe, campus police are visible, blue-light phones and escort services are readily available, and safety precautions are not overly necessary.

Computers

The Lowdown On...
Computers

High-Speed Network?
Yes

Number of Computers:
3,500

Wireless Network?
Yes

Operating Systems:
PC, Mac, UNIX

Number of Labs:
16 in dorms, 11 campus labs

Free Software:

Acrobat Reader	Mathematica
Antivirus software	Matlab
AutoCAD	Real Slideshow Basic
Groove	RealPlayer8Basic
ImageReady	SSH
Linux	Symantec Antivirus
Mac OS X amp	Telnet
Mallard, Banner	UI Direct
	WinZip 8.0

24-Hour Labs
All residence hall labs are open 24 hours a day.

Charge to Print?
Five cents a page.

Did You Know?
The residence halls have an online link that allows you to check what computers are open and what labs are full. Unfortunately, to check the link, you need a computer.

Students Speak Out On...
Computers

"The computer labs are decent. There are several located throughout campus. It's more convenient to have your own computer, although it is possible to get by without having your own."

Q "The computer labs are **kind of crowded**, but you can almost always find one to work at."

Q "I have my own computer, so I don't know much about the labs. I do go there sometimes, and **it doesn't seem too busy**. I think having or not having a computer does not really matter; each way works out."

Q "Yes, you should definitely take your own computer. The **lab areas are always crowded**. Noon is the worst time."

Q "I only know about the computer lab. But **they are always clean and in good condition**."

Q "The labs are no problem. **It does get busy**, but you can generally find a few open. I have never had to wait."

Q "There are plenty of computers. But **it is convenient to have one in your room** because a lot of classes are online now. So it is good to do classwork right next to your bed."

Q "**Sometimes the network is awful** because too many people are on the computer at the same time. However, I do not think that you would have to bring a computer, because there are always spaces available in the labs."

Q "The computer network is great. I did not have a computer for the first semester and the computer labs and printers worked fine. They are **not usually overly crowded**, and you can find a place to sit and work. The connections are pretty fast, and they all have the programs you will need and more."

Q "**The labs are good**. But it is better to have your own computer. Pray that your roommate does not have her own and uses the lab. Otherwise, you will hear her chatting online until four in the morning."

Q "Computer labs are generally pretty crowded, especially as the semester winds down. There are many computer facilities on campus though, including the English computer lab, which is open 24 hours a day. In the dorms **a network with fast connection is offered**."

Q "They did not lie when they said **U of I has computers everywhere on campus**. They are at the Union, in the library, at every residence hall, in some educational buildings. Even if you wanted to get away from them, you couldn't."

Q "You cannot go wrong if you decide to bring your own computer. You do not have to worry about crowded labs. But it can bring some of its own problems. Personal computers can act up, and when they do, you have to **find someone working in the computer lab to help you**."

Q "**There is the roommate situation to consider when it comes to computers**—if he/she does not have one, they may expect you to let them use yours all the time. I have seen the disastrous effects that can have on a human being."

Q "The dorm labs are always crowded on **a first-come, first-serve basis**, and there isn't a time limit or priority rating. That means if some geek wants to stay on for 72 hours; then, you are stuck waiting. Besides last year a kid was caught abusing himself to Internet pornography . . . eeewwww."

Q "Usually, **a lab is available somewhere**, but these labs have hours of operation which may be inconvenient. Students must also pay to print in the computer labs, which can be avoided by bringing a computer and printer."

Q "**Most students have personal computers** that connect to the Internet in their dorm room. This saves time and allows the student to use the computer labs as a back-up in case of problems with her or his machine, rather than be dependent on a lab that may have limited availability."

Q "I recommend having a computer, since many classes have online homework and quizzes. **The network is outstanding**. The Internet is super fast and great for downloading songs."

The College Prowler Take On...
Computers

Having your own omputer is a luxury at U of I—by no means a necessity—and several students feel that you don't have to bring your own. Are you so addicted to technology that you have to check your e-mail the second you get up? Are you going to hate shelling out a nickel for every page you print? Are you a fan of file-sharing and IMing? Those students who are, are glad that they brought their own computers with them. If you are not this type of student, then there is no need to spend money for your own computer, at least not while you are living in the dorms. You should know that the residence hall 24-hour labs are often loud areas, although they are supposed to be work stations. This makes it really difficult if you need quiet to work, so when writing a paper, you might want to vacate to labs that are not in the dorms. This is when most students say that having your own computer is handy.

A good thing about going to a state school is the funding, especially when this funding leads to great computer labs. The residence hall labs generally have a minimum of twenty computers, all with Internet access and a wide range of software; even though these labs are loud, they're adequately equipped. Although labs do get busy, it is rare for a computer to not to be available. Almost every main building has a computer lab, and depending on the time of day (early mornings and late nights are best), the labs can be open. A computer will always be available somewhere on campus; that, you can count on.

B

The College Prowler® Grade on

Computers: B

A high grade in Computers designates that computer labs are available, the computer network is easily accessible, and the campus' computing technology is up-to-date.

Facilities

The Lowdown On...
Facilities

Student Center:
The Illini Student Union

Athletic Centers:
Campus Recreation Center-East (Wimpe)
Ice arena
Intramural Physical Education building (IMPE)
Playing fields
Residence hall gyms

Libraries:
61

Campus Size:
1,454 acres

Popular Places to Chill:
Union
Espresso Royale
MPE

What Is There to Do on Campus?

The Quad is a hot spot on campus, especially in the warmer months. There is always a demonstration, charity event, or celebration taking place—or at the very least, a game of Frisbee. The shops on Green Street range from second-hand clothing stores to tattoo parlors. If this isn't your style, you can stop by IMPE (Intramural-Physical Education building) or Wimpe (nickname for Campus Recreations Center-East, or CRCE) for a workout or a swim. Krannert also stages plays regularly, ranging from classics like *Hamlet* to comedies like *Once Upon A Mattress*. Poetry and prose readings happen everywhere on campus, from Espresso Royale to the top floor of the school bookstore. Of course, the basement of the Union is the real social scene, equipped with a bowling alley, arcade, billiards, and snacks; it is a good place to waste a few hours.

Favorite Things to Do

The gyms are popular facilities and a good way to burn a few hours and calories. The coffeehouses around campus are also busy: some people drop by for a cup of coffee, others to chill with a friend, and some find it a good place to study. The Union is also a student favorite, as it offers good food, nice couches, a computer lab, a game room, and a small shop where you can buy everything from envelopes to chips. If the weather is nice, the Quad is also a comfortable hangout, and people sleep, study, and just generally relax in the grass.

Movie Theater on Campus?

Movies are occasionally shown at Gregory Hall, for a small price of $1 to $2 for U of I students.

Bowling on Campus?

Yes, in the Student Union.

Bar on Campus?

C.O. Daniels (Daniel Street)

Clybourne (Sixth Street)

It's Brothers

Joe's Brewery (Fifth Street)

Kam's

Legends (Green Street)

Murphy's

Station 211

Tonic (Wright Street)

Coffeehouse on Campus?

Espresso Royale (Illini Union)

Moonstruck (Wright Street)

Caffe Paradiso (Lincoln Avenue)

Students Speak Out On...
Facilities

{ **"The Union is pretty nice, and there are several places to stop and do homework or chill for a while. You can also grab some food when you don't want to go home to your dorm or apartment."**

Q "**The gym is nice**. They're adding on to it right now, so that's good."

Q "The gym was **small and annoying**, but now they are remodeling, which also kind of sucks."

Q "The athletic center, IMPE, is currently under construction and looks like it's going to be really nice in the coming fall. Otherwise, **it is very nice and has a lot of gym space** and good equipment."

Q "Altogether, the facilities are decent, but some leave definite things to be desired. The athletic facilities are **not adequate for such a large university**. Although, it must be said that improvements are being made."

Q "The gyms at the University are well-equipped with a large quantity and wide variety of aerobic machines and weight lifting equipment, but even with two separate facilities (IMPE and Wimpe), it can be hard to get a machine. **There is a sign-up process that reserves machines for students**, and it is best to get to the facility early to get what you want."

Q "The student union provides **a bowling alley and billiard room**, as well as an eatery with multicultural meal choices. There are several rooms for studying, coffee shops for fuel, Internet stations for checking e-mail on the UIUC server, ATM machines for convenient money withdrawal, and even the Courtyard Café where, at night, performances are given."

Q "As a member of the Big Ten, the facilities offered are very professional. The athletic facilities are the place where Division I Big Ten contenders in every sport practice, though the gym gets crowded at times. The library is the third largest library in the country (after Harvard and Yale) and **the most accessible in the world**."

Q "The center of University activities is the Union, a building between the main Quad and Engineering Quad. Aside from **study areas and a coffee shop**, there are restaurants, a pool, and a bowling alley available."

Q "IMPE and Wimpe are the most popular fitness centers on campus and can be reached through the bus line and are also **within a comfortable walking distance** from every residence hall."

Q "Everything on campus is **pretty much the best there is available**. Some of our alumni include Roger Ebert and Hugh Hefner, so we get a lot of financial support. As a matter of fact, after winter break of the 2001–2002 school year during which our football team competed in the Nokia Sugar Bowl, we had brand new public buses on campus."

Q "The Illini Union is one of the most popular places because it is located on the Quad, the center of the campus and surrounded by residence and educational halls. **I love it because it has everything**. If I am hungry, I can choose between a Big Mac or orange chicken. If I am thirsty and need to stay up for the night, I can sip a café latte while studying in the Courtyard Café."

Q "The whole university is very well run and very well organized. **Everything is easily accessible** and, for the most part, the staff is extremely helpful."

Q "There are instrument practice rooms in every dorm, as well as **furnished lounges and ping pong, pool and foosball tables**."

The College Prowler Take On...
Facilities

U of I's campus has many places to keep students busy with daytime and evening activities. During the day at the Illini Union, students lounge between classes and eat in the basement food court, with a variety of food from Chinese to McDonald's to Blimpie. The student bank and computer lab are here, too, which is convenient for students who want to get work done between classes. In the Union's basement, the bowling alleys and the billiards area are student favorites, but the arcade is popular, too, as it offers even the trendiest new games, like Dance Dance Revolution. For students who don't want to spend their nights at a bar, the Union is definitely the place to be. The gyms also attract many students; they're up to par for Division I Big Ten athletes, but even the athletically inclined like to chill there. Coffeehouses are always popular, especially the ones next to campus. Some even offer wireless hookups, which makes them a great place for students to work and relax.

Beyond the gyms and arcade, the University's greatest features are its beautiful buildings and grounds. From Foellinger Auditorium to the English Building, the buildings are aestheticially pleasing and interesting. The Quad is a wide expanse of well-manicured grass and trees. Lined by striking brick buildings on all sides, the Quad maintains a classic feel with its tree-lined walkways, crisscrossed sidewalks, and the Eternal Flame bench for lovers. Students at U of I enjoy all the facilities the University has to offer, both in and out of doors.

The College Prowler® Grade on

Facilities: A-

A high Facilities grade indicates that the campus is aesthetically pleasing and well-maintained; facilities are state-of-the-art, and libraries are exceptional. Other determining factors include the quality of both athletic and student centers and an abundance of things to do on campus.

Campus Dining

The Lowdown On...
Campus Dining

Freshman Meal Plan Requirement?
Yes

Meal Plan Average Cost:
$3,570

Places to Grab a Bite with Your Meal Plan

A La Carte

Locations: Forbes (day), Illinois Avenue Hall (day and night), Pennsylvania Avenue Hall (night), Busey-Evans Hall (night), Peabody (night)

Food: American

Favorite Dish: Pizza

Hours: Hours vary from hall to hall for each A La Carte location. Check out *www.housing.uiuc.edu/dining/locations.asp* for details.

Blimpie

Location: Union, lower level

Food: Sub sandwiches

Favorite Dish: Steak and onion melt

Hours: Mon-Fri: 11 a.m.–7 p.m.

Cactus Grill

Location: Union, lower level

Food: American

Favorite Dish: Potato wedges

Hours: Monday–Thursday 10 a.m.–7 p.m., Friday 10 a.m.–4 p.m., Saturday 11 a.m.–2 p.m.

Cocina Mexicana

Location: Illinois Avenue Hall

Food: Mexican

Favorite Dish: Steak fajitas

Hours: Friday 4:45 p.m.–7 p.m.

Delights!

Location: Union, main level

Food: Ice cream/baked goods

Favorite Dish: Frozen yogurt

Hours: Monday–Thursday 7:30 a.m.–10 p.m., Friday 7:30 a.m.–6 p.m., Saturday–Sunday 12 noon-6 p.m.

Espresso Royale

Location: Union, main level

Food: Coffee, sandwiches

Favorite Dish: Cherry danish

Hours: Monday–Friday 7 a.m.–11 p.m., Saturday–Sunday 8 a.m.–11 p.m., Sunday–10:30 a.m.–7 p.m.

Fat Don's

Location: Pennsylvania Avenue Hall

Food: American

Favorite Dish: Big baked potatoes

Hours: Wednesday 4:30 p.m.–7 p.m.

Field of Greens

Location: Lincoln Avenue Hall

Food: Vegetarian

Favorite Dish: Soy pasta

Hours: Monday–Friday 11 a.m.–1:15 p.m.

Illini Orange Store

Location: 301 E. Gregory

Food: Snacks, groceries, baked goods

Favorite Dish: Donuts

Hours: Monday–Friday 9:30 a.m.–11 p.m., Saturday–Sunday 12 noon-11 p.m.

Illini Union Ballroom

Location: Union, second level

Food: Variety buffet

Favorite Dish: Pasta primavera

Hours: Monday–Friday 11:30 a.m.–1:30 p.m.

Illini Union Vending Room

Location: Main level

Food: Chips, candy, muffins, bagels

Favorite Dish: Doritos

Hours: Daily 7 a.m.–3 a.m.

Italian Kitchen

Location: Gregory Drive

Food: Italian

Favorite Dish: Cannoli

Hours: Friday 5 p.m.–7 p.m.

McDonald's

Location: Union, lower level

Food: American

Favorite Dish: Chicken McNuggets

Hours: Monday–Friday 7 a.m.–11 p.m., Saturday–Sunday 8 a.m.–11 p.m.

Oodles

Location: Busey-Evans Hall

Food: Variety buffet

Favorite Dish: Couscous

Hours: Friday 11 a.m.–1:30 p.m.

Quad Shop

Location: Union, main level

Food: Snacks and sundries

Favorite Dish: Fresh popcorn

Hours: Everyday 7 a.m.–10 p.m.

Rice Garden

Location: Union, lower level

Food: Chinese

Favorite Dish: Egg rolls

Hours: Monday–Thursday 10 a.m.–7 p.m., Friday 10 a.m.–3:30 p.m., Saturday 11 a.m.–3 p.m.

Sbarro

Location: Union, lower level

Food: Italian pizzeria

Favorite Dish: Cheese pizza

Hours: Monday–Thursday 10 a.m.–7 p.m., Friday 10 a.m.–4 p.m., Saturday 11 a.m.– 2:30 p.m.

Soul Ingredient

Location: Florida Avenue Hall

Food: Southern cooking

Favorite Dish: Cornbread

Hours: Thursday 4:45 p.m.–7:30 p.m.

Sushi San

Location: Union, lower level

Food: Sushi

Favorite Dish: Shrimp sushi

Hours: Monday–Thursday 10 a.m.–7 p.m., Friday 10 a.m.–3:30 p.m., Saturday 11 a.m.–3 p.m.

Off-Campus Places to Use Your Meal Plan:
None.

24-Hour On-Campus Eating?
No, but Merry-Ann's Diner is located nearby.

Student Favorites
A La Carte

Fat Don's

Sbarro

Other Options

Some students choose to skip dinner and instead have a pizza delivered to their room later that night. It counts as a meal and most students agree it is better than eating in the cafeteria.

Did You Know?

During Finals Week, the residence hall cafeterias host **snacks and drinks for late-night studiers**. Some even offer Midnight Breakfast, a full course complete with French toast and pancakes. It is a tradition that should not be missed.

Students Speak Out On...
Campus Dining

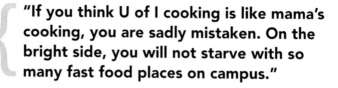

"If you think U of I cooking is like mama's cooking, you are sadly mistaken. On the bright side, you will not starve with so many fast food places on campus."

Q "Lunch and breakfast in the dining halls are good. Dinner is bad. As for outside the dorms, **there is a good selection of food on campus.**"

Q "The food in the dining halls is gross. They feed you **the same thing every night**, over and over again."

Q "I never ate in the dining halls, but I hear they are really bad. **Campus eating is okay**, but it is so hard to find food that isn't greasy."

Q "There are some meals that are decent, but others are like **experiments gone wrong.**"

Q "Sometimes you just wish they would feed you regular food whenever they try to get fancy with something like 'nut-crusted loin' . . . well, **thank God for delivery pizza**."

Q "**The food is cafeteria food** . . . what else can I say?"

Q "The **cafeteria food is not as bad as it may seem**. I complained while I was living in the dorms of course, but now that I am off campus, I know that it was a blessing."

Q "The UC and the Six-Pack are pretty good. And ISR is right next to the Quad so **it is easy to grab lunch there between classes**."

Q "The cafeterias are **pretty much the same all over campus**—bad. Some of the hours differ, though; some are more flexible."

Q "College life in general is notorious for lack of good food, and the University of Illinois dining services is no different. However, what it might lack in first-class food, it makes up in offering a variety of choices. Though one might not get their first choice, **there will always be something to eat in the dorms**."

Q "The dorms at UIUC offer specialty restaurants on certain nights of the week. On regular nights, even if the hot food isn't appealing, there is always cereal, bagels, and sandwich makings to ensure that no one goes hungry. **The Edy's ice cream machines are also a big hit**."

Q "Students do go wild over specialty restaurants that are held in different dorms like Wok on the Wild Side (Asian cuisine), Soul Ingredient (soul food), and the favorite: Fat Don's, where they serve steaks (and let me tell you, those steaks they serve are **big, juicy, and tender**)."

Q "During weekend afternoons, the dining halls are packed, and its gets a little annoying trying to maneuver around or wait for more chicken and fries, because **they run out of everything**."

Q "Sure, **the food sucks**. But look on the bright side: now you know how astronauts feel. Except they get Tang. We don't. Hey, that sucks!"

Q "Campus dining in the dorms is not something you want to do; it's something that you have to do when you don't have money. The up side to the situation is that **once a week a local restaurant goes to every dorm** on campus and prepares something special to break the monotony of the slimy beef stroganoff that slightly resembles vomit. There is nothing wrong with eating genetically-modified vegetables . . . right?"

Q "The food on campus is not horrible, though sometimes we all wonder. The best dorms to eat at are ISR, Busey-Evans, and LAR. The best meals are lunch where they serve the basics. At supper, they usually try to mix things up with food I have never heard of before, and **they always have pasta, pasta, pasta.**"

Q "**Keep canned food in your room for emergencies.** Also, ramen has saved me a couple of nights. Also, sometimes I skip the cafeteria line and head straight for the vending machine line—which is usually more popular."

Q "The food is not of the best quality. **The ISR cafeteria is good.** But you can never know what is good, the way they prepare the food."

The College Prowler Take On...
Campus Dining

College is often well-known for two things: parties and bad food. The dining halls leave much to be desired. Most students agree that instead of working hard to make creative new foods and variety, the University should just stick to learning how to make Rice Krispie treats properly. Cafeteria food is always going to be cafeteria food, which means either boring repetition or outlandish creations that make you skip right to the cereal bar. Keeping the food fresh is also a problem, as students who have eaten slimy lettuce or stale Cheerios can tell you. It is a good idea to come early to take advantage of the fresh food. On the other hand, the hours can also be a problem. Most students do not like eating dinner by 6:30 p.m., especially when they are going to be up until 2 a.m. studying. Consequently, most dorm rooms are stocked with snacks and sodas.

7 Specialty restaurants like A La Carte offer better food at more reasonable hours. When you are up late studying or just hanging out, there is nothing better than pizza or onion rings at Illinois Avenue Residence Hall. If it was not for specialty restaurants, the dining at U of I would be bleak. Even with these options, the University must work on its healthy food menu, as most main courses and appetizers are all simmering in grease and fat. Also, the vegetarian fare is limited to pasta and salads in most residence halls, which is less than tempting. All in all, the dining experience at U of I is stereotypically bad.

D

The College Prowler® Grade on
Campus Dining: D

Our grade on Campus Dining addresses the quality of both school-owned dining halls and independent on-campus restaurants as well as the price, availability, and variety of food.

Off-Campus Dining

The Lowdown On...
Off-Campus Dining

Restaurant Prowler:
Popular Places to Eat!

Biaggi's Ristorante Italiano
Food: Italian
2235 S. Neil Street
(217) 356-4300
Price: $15 and under
per person
Hours: Monday–Thursday
11 a.m.–10 p.m., Friday–
Saturday 11 a.m.–11 p.m.,
Sunday 11 a.m.–9 p.m.

Bonnie Jean's
Food: American
901 S. Fourth Street
(217) 239-2121
Price: $10 and under
per person
Hours: Monday–Sunday
11 a.m.–2 a.m.

Courier Café
Food: American
111 N. Race Street, Urbana
(217) 328-1811
Price: $10 and under
per person
Hours: Sunday–Thursday
7 a.m.–11 p.m., Friday–
Saturday 7 a.m.–12 p.m.

Dos Reales Mexican Restaurant

Food: Mexican

1407 N. Prospect

(217) 351-6879

Price: $12 and under
per person

Hours: Monday–Thursday
11 a.m.–10 p.m., Friday–
Saturday 11 a.m.–12 p.m.,
Sunday 11 a.m.–8 p.m.

Empire Chinese Restaurant

Food: Asian

410 E. Green

(217) 328-0832

Price: $15 and under
per person

Hours: Monday–Saturday
11 a.m.–10:30 p.m., Sunday
11 a.m.–9 p.m.

Fat City Saloon and Grill

Food: Bar and Grill

505 S. Chestnut

(217) 356-7100

Price: $10 and under
per person

Hours: Daily 11 a.m.–2 a.m.

Gumby's Pizza

Food: Pizza

1409 S. Neil Street

(217) 355-3278

Price: $8 and under per person

Hours: Daily 11 a.m.–3 a.m.

Jupiter's

Food: American

39 E. Main

(217) 398-5988

Price: $10 and under
per person

Hours: Monday–Saturday
11 a.m.–2 a.m., Sunday
12 p.m.–2 a.m.

Kamakura Japanese

Food: Japanese

715 S. Neil Street

(217) 351-9898

Price: $15 and under
per person

Hours: Monday–Friday 5 p.m.–
10 p.m., Saturday 12 p.m.–
10 p.m., Sunday 4 p.m.–9 p.m.

Kennedy's at Stone Creek

Food: American/Fine Dining

2560 S. Stone Creek

(217) 384-8111

Price: $15 and under
per person

Hours: Monday–Saturday
10 a.m.–10 p.m., Sunday
9 a.m.–8 p.m.

La Bamba

Food: Mexican

313 N. Mathis

(217) 355-2888

Price $5 and under per person

Hours: Monday–Thursday
11 a.m.–10 p.m., Friday–
Saturday 11 a.m.–3 a.m.,
Sunday 11 a.m.–9 p.m.

Mandarin Wok
Food: Asian
403 E. Green
(217) 337-1200
Price: $10 and under
per person
Hours: Monday–Saturday
11 a.m.–9 p.m., Sunday
11 a.m.–6 p.m.

Merry-Ann's Diner
Food: Breakfast
1510 S. Neil Street
(217) 352-5399
Price: $10 and under
per person
Hours: Daily 24 hours

Papa Del's Pizza
Food: Pizzeria
206 E. Green Street
(217) 359-7700
Price: $10 and under
per person
Hours: Monday–Saturday
11 a.m.–12:30 p.m., Sunday
11 a.m.–11 p.m.

Radio Maria
Food: American
119 N. Walnut
(217) 398-7729
Price: $10 and under
per person
Hours: Sunday–Friday 11 a.m.–
2:30 p.m., Monday–Friday
5 p.m.–10 p.m.

Red Herring
Food: Vegetarian
1209 W. Oregon, Urbana
(217) 367-2340
Price: $10 and under
per person
Hours: Monday–Friday
11 a.m.–3 p.m., Monday
5:30 p.m.–7:30 p.m.

Red Lobster
Food: Seafood
1901 N. Prospect Avenue
(217) 355-2577
Price: $15 and under
per person
Hours: Sunday–Thursday
11 a.m.–10 p.m., Saturday–
Friday 11 a.m.–10 p.m.

Strawberry Fields
Food: Vegetarian
306 W. Springfield, Urbana
(217) 328-1655
Price: $10 and under
per person
Hours: Monday–Saturday
7 a.m.–8 p.m., Sunday
2 p.m.–6 p.m.

Za's
Food: Italian
2006 W. Springfield Avenue
(217) 355-4990
Price: $10 and under
per person
Hours: Monday–Saturday
11 a.m.–9:30 p.m., Sunday
11 a.m.–9 p.m.

Zorba's

Food: Greek

627 E. Green Street

(217) 344-0710

Price: $10 and under
per person

Hours: Monday–Thursday
11 a.m.–10 p.m., Friday–
Saturday 11 a.m.–12 p.m.,
Sunday 11 a.m.–9 p.m.

Closest Grocery Stores:

Country Market
1914 Glen Park Dr.
(217) 356-8242

Jerry's IGA
312 W. Kirby Avenue
(217) 352-0019

Meijer
2401 N. Prospect
(217) 355-3801

Student Favorites:

Kennedy's at Stone Creek
Mandarin Wok
Radio Maria
Za's

Late-Night, Half-Price Food Specials:

Gumby's
La Bamba

24-Hour Eating:

Merry-Ann's Diner

Best Pizza:
Papa Del's Pizza

Best Chinese:
Mandarin Wok

Best Breakfast:
Merry-Ann's Diner

Best Wings:
Fat City Saloon and Grill

Best Healthy:
Strawberry Fields

Best Place to Take Your Parents:
Kennedy's at Stone Creek

Other Places to Check Out:
Brothers
Burger King
Cheddar's
Garcia's
Giovanni's
Jarling's Custard Cup
Jimmy John's
McDonald's
Minneci's
Monical's
Oakley
Perkins
Pita Pit
Steak n' Shake
Subway
White Horse

Did You Know?

Illinois was home to **the first McDonald's** restaurant. **Popcorn has finally been voted the official snack** food of Illinois after years of heated debate.

If you ask for soda in this town, you will be laughed right out of the restaurant. The only word used around here is "pop."

Popcorn has finally been voted the official snack food of Illinois after years of heated debate.

If you ask for soda in this town, you will be laughed right out of the restaurant. The only word used around here is "pop."

Students Speak Out On...
Off-Campus Dining

"There are tons of restaurants off campus including the usual chains, but one of my favorites is the Courier on Race Street. It is in downtown Urbana and has good hamburgers, appetizers, and desserts."

Q "**Restaurants off campus are great**, especially those which are found at Baytowne, i.e. Cheddar's."

Q "Restaurants off campus are good. I guess I heard that **Champaign has the second most restaurants per capita in the country**. The good spots are Dos Reales, Minneci's, and the Courier Café."

Q "I eat at **Jimmy John's, Gumby's, and Za's**. They are my favorites."

Q "I like to eat at Giovanni's on campus, which has good food. I have never been to any of the off-campus restaurants. I don't have a car and **they are too far away**."

Q "I don't know about food off campus too much. I think **on campus is more convenient** 'cause its closer."

Q "**Off-campus eating is too far away**. I only eat on campus, which isn't too bad. It is easy to walk to places."

Q "Off-campus restaurants are **not as readily available as they would be in the city**, however there are many choices. Aside from the usual chain restaurants like Red Lobster, there are independent locations like Oakley and Perkins, which are diners off campus. Custard Cup, a seasonally-open ice cream parlor, is considered by many to offer the best ice cream they've ever tasted."

Q "Next to campus, within walking distance, there are a variety of restaurants on Green Street. The food there ranges **from chains like Subway and Burger King to independent places** like Pita Pit and Zorba's."

Q "If you get tired of dorm food, you can eat out. In Champaign and within the shopping vicinity, students can eat at Red Lobster or Steak N' Shake. **Near campus, places like McDonald's close around 11 p.m. daily**."

Q "If you want a taste of something different, the Pita Pit and Papa John's are good places. **A lot of restaurants also deliver**, even late into the night with pizza and good spicy chicken at Gumby's."

Q "**The restaurants in Champaign have a pretty good selection**. The more popular ventures are the various wing nights. The White Horse offers a Tuesday night wing special of a pound of wings for $2.50, which is about ten wings. Brothers has ten cent wings on Thursday nights. Pizza is a big deal on campus, too. Some of the hot spots include Garcia's, Gumby's (the pokey sticks are legendary), Bonnie Jean's (post-bar by the slice specialty), Papa Del's, and Monical's."

Q "There are a variety of restaurants that serve Asian food, from Chinese to Korean, Japanese, Cantonese, and Thai. In C-U, there is **a restaurant for every palate**."

Q "You've got your basics like Red Lobster and Burger King. But then you also have **unique stuff like Zorba's**. And of course, college is probably the only place in the world where you can order pizza at two in the morning."

The College Prowler Take On...
Off-Campus Dining

While dining in the residence halls can be a problem, off-campus dining is guaranteed to make you gain some of that Freshman 15. There are restaurants all over Green Street, from the most predictable like Burger King and Subway, to the out of the ordinary like Zorba's or Red Herring. There is Mexican, Greek, Italian, Chinese, Japanese, seafood, and fine dining—most within a few miles of campus. However, some of the chains or high-end restaurants are not located near campus, which can be problem. If you have a yearning for Red Lobster, you will have to choose between an extensive bus ride or carpool. However, most students, especially freshmen, find it easier to eat the variety of food on campus. And of course, there is always pizza to rely on.

On weekends, Gumby's delivers up until 3 a.m., a fact everyone in college takes advantage of once in a while. Every Tuesday night, Gumby's has a buy one get one free Pokey Sticks sale that is a must. Nevertheless, eating healthy can be a problem. There are places like Red Herring and Strawberry Fields that cater to vegetarians and those on a healthy diet, but for the most part, off-campus dining is heavy in grease and calories. Another problem is the distance to the grocery stores. If you live in the residence halls but still want to stock up on food and drinks, you are going to have to either take the bus or walk. The best grocery store, Mejier's, is nowhere near Green Street, so if you want more than Hostess and Doritos, you are going to have to forget County Market and take a long bus ride.

B

The College Prowler® Grade on

**Off-Campus
Dining: B**

A high Off-Campus Dining grade implies that off-campus restaurants are affordable, accessible, and worth visiting. Other factors include the variety of cuisine and the availability of alternative options (vegetarian, vegan, Kosher, etc.).

Campus Housing

The Lowdown On...
Campus Housing

Undergrads Living on Campus:
30%

Number of Dormitories:
23

Number of University-Owned Apartments:
18

Best Dorms:
Lincoln Avenue Residence Halls

The Six-Pack (Garner, Weston, Snyder, Lundgren, Taft-Van Doren)

Illinois Residence Halls

Worst Dorms:
Florida Avenue Residence Hall (FAR)

Pennsylvania Residence Halls (PAR)

Dormitories:

Allen

Floors: 4 floors, plus ground floor

Total Occupancy: 650

Bathrooms: Shared by floor

Coed: Yes

Residents: Mostly freshmen, sophomores, juniors, seniors

Room Types: Double, triple, quad

Special Features: Ceramics studio, darkroom, classrooms, computer center

Busey-Evans

Floors: 4

Total Occupancy: 400

Bathrooms: Shared by floor

Coed: No, all female

Residents: Freshmen, sophomores, juniors, seniors

Room Types: double

Special Features: A/C, meeting spaces, classrooms, study areas, computer lab

Florida Avenue (FAR)

Floors: 12

Total Occupancy: 1241

Bathrooms: Shared by floor

Coed: Yes

Residents: Mostly freshmen, sophomores, juniors, seniors

Room Types: single, double, triple

Special Features: A/C, close to student parking lot, exercise room, computer lab, library, two dining rooms

Gregory Drive

Floors: 5 four-story buildings

Total Occupancy: 1700

Bathrooms: Shared by floor

Coed: Yes, Forbes, Garner, and Hopkins Halls—Barton is all female and Lundgren is all male

Residents: Freshmen, sophomores, juniors, seniors

Room Types: Single, double, triple

Special Features: Library, computer center, exercise room, music practice rooms, recreation fields nearby

Illinois Avenue

Floors: 12 (women tower), 5 (men tower)

Total Occupancy: 1200

Bathrooms: Shared by floor

Coed: Yes, women's tower and men's tower

Residents: Mostly freshmen, sophomores, juniors, seniors

Room Types: Double, triple, large triple, corner triple

Special Features: A/C, darkroom, computer center, lounges, across from Krannert Center of Performing Arts, close to Quad

→

Lincoln Avenue

Floors: 4, plus basement

Total Occupancy: 460

Bathrooms: Shared by floor

Coed: No, all female

Residents: Mostly freshmen, sophomores, juniors, seniors

Room Types: Single, double, corner double, triple

Special Features: Grand piano, music practice rooms, vending room, library, pool table, ping pong table, two dining halls, computer lab

Peabody Avenue (Six-Pack)

Floors: 5, 4 in Scott

Bathrooms: Shared by floor

Coed: Yes, Taft, Van Doren: coed layered; Scott, Snyder, Weston, Garner: coed split (men and women on different floors)

Residents: Mostly freshmen, sophomores, juniors, seniors

Room Types: Double, large double, corner triple, triple

Special Features: Library, computer center, darkroom, game room, exercise room, music room, lounges

Pennsylvania Avenue (PAR)

Floors: 4

Total Occupancy: 1024

Bathrooms: Shared by floor

Coed: Yes

Residents: Mostly freshmen, sophomores, juniors, seniors

Room Types: Double

Special Features: Library, close to student parking lot, game room, exercise room, music room, lounges, darkroom, computer lab

Private Certified Housing:

Armory House

Floors: 3 in the main area, 5 in the suites

Total Occupancy: 120

Bathrooms: Private, semi-private

Coed: Yes

Residents: Mostly freshmen, sophomores, juniors, seniors

Room Types: Single, double, deluxe double

Special Features: Weekly housekeeping service, secured accesses to entrances and parking, A/C, carpeted suites, large private baths, comfortable floor lounges

→

Brown House on Coler

Floors: 1

Total Occupancy: 4

Coed: No, all male

Special Features: Academic atmosphere, neat, near campus, residential community

Bromley Hall

Floors: 13

Total Occupancy: 712

Bathrooms: Private, semi-private

Coed: Yes

Residents: Mostly freshmen, sophomores, juniors, seniors

Room Types: Single, double, triple

Special Features: Housekeeping service, A/C, large heated indoor swimming pool, largest rooms on campus, central computer lab, two laundromats, baby grand piano

Christian Campus House

Floors: 2

Total Occupancy: 11

Coed: No, all male

Special Features: Free laundry, communal cooking, leadership events, interview mandatory

Europa House

Floors: 4

Total Occupancy: 88

Bathrooms: Semi-private

Coed: Yes

Residents: Freshmen, sophomores, juniors, seniors

Room Types: Apartment-style, 2 doubles in each suite

Special Features: Parking garage, security entrance, swimming pool, fireplace, satellite reception, contemporary furniture, double the floor space of dorms, balcony off each room

Hendrick House

Floors: 10

Total Occupancy: 364

Bathrooms: Semi-private

Coed: Yes, but mostly male

Residents: Mostly freshmen, sophomores, juniors, seniors

Room Types: East double, west double, east single, west single

Special Features: Weekly housekeeping, strict quiet hours, exercise room, pool tables, off-street parking, individual Ethernet connections

Illini Tower

Floors: 15

Total Occupancy: 710

Bathrooms: Semi-private

Coed: Yes

Residents: Mostly freshmen, sophomores, juniors, seniors

Room Types: 2-bedroom, 4-person apartments, efficiencies, 3- and 4-bedroom apartments

Special Features: Weekly housekeeping, resident-controlled A/C, 24-hour quiet study lounge, cable TV, music room, game room, furnished kitchen and living room for each 4-person apartment

Koinonia Christian Cooperative

Floors: 3

Total Occupancy: 35

Coed: No, all male

Special Features: Baptist affiliation

McKinley Men's Residence Hall

Floors: 2

Total Occupancy: 7

Coed: No, all male

Special Features: Self-governing, meals and housekeeping by residents, close to Quad, no alcohol and no smoking, sponsored by Presbyterian Ministry

Nabor House Fraternity

Floors: 3

Total Occupancy: 40

Coed: No, all male

Room Types: Single, double, triple

Special Features: Agricultural backgrounds and majors for all residents, high GPAs, intramural sports teams

Nevada House

Floors: 2

Total Occupancy: 15

Bathrooms: Semi-private

Coed: No, all women

Room Types: Singles

Special Features: Self-governed, quiet residential area, available parking, washer/dryer, color TV

Newman Hall

Floors: 4

Total Occupancy: 288

Bathrooms: Semi-private

Coed: Yes

Residents: Freshmen, sophomores, juniors, seniors

Special Features: Close to quad, bed linens, cable TV, ceiling fans, large desks, optional parking, computer lab, library, lounges

Newman House

Floors: 3

Total Occupancy: 39

Bathrooms: Semi-private

Coed: No, all female

Room Types: Single or apartment-style

Special Features: Housekeeping, bed linens, carpeted, parking, close to Quad, laundry on site

Presby House

Floors: 2

Total Occupancy: 30

Bathrooms: Shared by floor

Coed: No, all female

Residents: Mostly freshmen, sophomores, juniors, seniors

Room Types: Double

Special Features: Self-governed, "Big Sister" program to help new students, high involvement in offices and community services, grand piano, laundry, kitchen access, computer lab, parking

Stratford House

Floors: 2

Total Occupancy: 30

Bathrooms: Shared by floor

Coed: No, all female

Residents: Mostly freshmen, sophomores, juniors, seniors

Room Types: Double

Special Features: Home-style atmosphere, chores and meals done by residents, Christian affiliation, cable TV, washers, dryers, music room, close to campus

University YMCA

Floors: Third floor for residents

Total Occupancy: 12

Coed: No, all male

Special Features: A/C, VCR/DVD, computer, across from Quad, free laundry, parking

Housing Offered:

Singles: 7%

Doubles: 88%

Triples/Suites: 5%

Bed Type
Twin extra-long, some lofts, some bunk beds

Available for Rent
Mini fridge with microwave

What You Get
Bed, desk, chair, blinds, dresser, one mirror, free local phone calls, cable TV and dorm movie channel, Ethernet connection, closet, storage drawer under bed

Also Available
Smoke-free living, substance-free living, non-visitation communities (no male visitors), Living/Learning communities

Room Types
Residence hall rooms include doubles, quads, singles, triples, and corner doubles. All residence hall bathrooms are public and shared by a wing. Hence one floor will generally have two bathrooms, one for each wing.

Private certified housing, on the other hand, generally offers its residents private or semi-private bathrooms. Private housing generally comes with many more amenities, although they also tend to be more expensive.

Coed split dorms are halls that have men and women living on the same floor, although in different wings. Coed layered dorms have men and women living on separate floors.

Cleaning Service?
Only in public areas, unless otherwise noted in private certified housing. Bathrooms and other areas are cleaned daily by staff in residence halls.

Did You Know?

Living/Learning communities give residents a chance to expand their horizons. There are five sections that seek to reach out to all types of students: Global Crossroads; Unit One; Weston Exploration; Women in Math, Science, and Engineering; and Leadership Experience through Academic Development and Service.

All residence hall students have a dorm movie channel which plays three to four recent movies a day. The movies change about once a month.

Go online to *www.housing.uiuc.edu/living/llc/index.asp* to find out more.

Students Speak Out On...
Campus Housing

"Live in the Six-Pack [Peabody Avenue] if you want to live in the dorms. People are actually social there, not geeky. You will meet more people in the Six-Pack and have more fun."

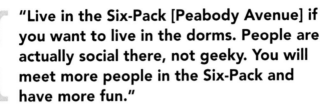

Q "I stayed in Bromley, and **it was nice and clean**. I never really heard about bad dorms here."

Q "I hear **some of the dorms are pretty small**. I live right next to the Quad, so that's cool. Some dorms are bad though; people pull the fire alarms all night long. At least, that hasn't happened to me yet."

Q "Illini Street Residence (ISR) is the best dorm, but not many freshmen are placed at ISR. The Six-Pack, a set of six dorms in Champaign, is where many freshmen end up staying. The dorms there are nothing special, a little smaller than the other dorms, but definitely livable."

Q "The Six-Pack is honestly **the best place to live**. Stay away from FAR though. Avoid it if you can."

Q "I have only lived at Scott. But **I liked it**; there are a lot of Asians here."

Q "**I am moving out of Synder**. That is all I have to say."

Q "I only lived in the dorms one year, but **I had a good time** and I met a lot of people."

Q "The Six-Pack is good. It is **very social**, and you always have fun."

Q "The dorms vary. **They can be very different experiences**. PAR has an open and closed lounge. It is nice but there are no triples. The Six-Pack dorms have triples, though. And the tunnels are nice."

Q "Know that when you come to U of I, **it is not going to be home**, but as they say, a home away from home. It will take a lot of adjusting to, for example, the floormates, the roommate, and the bathroom, and just the whole facility. That is why it is so important to do the research so that you can pick a place that is best suited for you and your needs."

Q "I have not heard too much about private housing, but regular campus residence halls fare just as well because they are located close to classes and have **the services that freshmen need to help them adjust**."

Q "If you like noise, **live in the Six-Pack**; if you don't, enough said. If you want to be close to your classes and in a coed building, Illinois Street Residence Hall may be for you—and like FAR, it has air conditioning."

Q "Most students are faced with either going to **a public dorm or private dorm**. Two of the most popular private dorms are Illini Towers, which is predominantly Jewish, and Bromley."

Q "Your best bet is living in a setting where you feel you can succeed, and the University of Illinois provides that. **Quieter dorms, partying dorms, and everywhere in between**—pick one and make the best of it."

Q "In general, the closer you are to your classes the better off you are going to be, so **try and live somewhere near where your classes are**. Engineers: ISR. Liberal Arts: Six-Pack. People that get stuck there: FAR/PAR."

Q "**The most popular place to be freshman year is the Six-Pack**, located in the center of campus closest to the Memorial Football Stadium and Assembly Hall Basketball Arena. It's not as nice as the private dorms, but it's socially the best bet. Most people will tell you that by their senior year, their best friends are people that they met in the Six-Pack as freshmen."

Q "In general, the University-owned dorms look like a mistake from some 1960's architectural experiment gone horribly wrong. **They are very utilitarian**, but at the same time, it is what you make of them that counts. My experience in the dorms was a very positive one and the buildings are not what matter, but rather the people you surround yourself with."

Q "**If you like the smell of cow crap**, live at FAR. Mmm, good."

Q "**Don't go all-girls**. Don't live in Urbana."

The College Prowler Take On...
On-Campus Housing

Housing at college can often be a nightmare. Luckily, the University offers many options for its students, which means that almost anyone can find a place to make them happy. Each dorm has its pluses and minuses, and several students have experienced the good and bad of each residence hall at some point. On the plus side, FAR/PAR are the only dorms that are close to the student parking lot. Lincoln Avenue and Busey-Evans Residence Halls are the two women-only dorms, and students say they are also the cleanest and most aesthetically pleasing. The Six-Pack is a collection of six dorms beside one another. They are allegedly the wildest of the dorms, perhaps because they have many freshmen in close together, but they are great dorms to make friends freshman year.

The drawbacks to campus housing are that some halls are too far from the Quad, have limited space, offer no parking, and very few have air-conditioning. However, they all offer dining halls (students say ISR is the best), laundry, and computer labs. But this is all relative to what you make out of your hall experience. Private certified housing is another popular option among students even though it may come at a slightly higher price. This housing has the most and the best amenities and is an example of how campus housing ranges from the bare basics to pretty darn nice. Campus housing can shape your social and academic habits, so choose wisely, or try to adjust well to what you're assigned to.

B-

The College Prowler® Grade on

Campus Housing: B-

A high Campus Housing grade indicates that dorms are clean, well-maintained, and spacious. Other determining factors include variety of dorms, proximity to classes, and social atmosphere.

Off-Campus Housing

The Lowdown On...
Off-Campus Housing

Undergrads in Off-Campus Housing:
70%

Average Rent For:
Studio Apt.: $450/month
1BR Apt.: $550/month
2BR Apt.: $600/month

Popular Areas:
Green Street
Wright Street
Fourth Street
Mattis Avenue

Best Time to Look For a Place:
Beginning of second semester

For Assistance Contact

Student Tenant Union (Room 326, Illini Union)
www.tenantunion.uiuc.edu

(217) 333-0112

E-mail: certhsg@uiuc.edu

www.community.housing.uiuc.edu

Students Speak Out On...
Off-Campus Housing

"I am getting an apartment next year. It is pretty close and cheap. It is almost the same cost as the dorm, considering the housing increase."

Q "**Off-campus housing is worth it**, if that's what you are looking for. I wish it wasn't so expensive though."

Q "**Getting an apartment in one's freshman year is nearly out of the question**. If there is a need to get an apartment, one can petition to get out of the requirement to stay in the dorm or private housing."

Q "After one year in the dorms, most people can't wait to get out. The property companies create this false rush to make it seem like all the good places will be gone if you don't sign by Thanksgiving. That is all wrong. **One year, I found a great place in June** for only $187 a month."

Q "The hard part is dealing with these companies who barely clean the apartment before you move in and are extremely slow to fix problems with the place. **They will keep your security deposit if the faucet doesn't run right**. They really try to take you through the ringer, so you have to be careful. But after being in the dorms, you'll do anything for your own room. Big balconies are all the rage, and if you can find five people, renting a house is a pretty good deal as well."

Q "All I can say is, **try to live as close to the Quad as possible**. Cheap rent is good, but nothing makes up for a long walk to class in the freezing cold. Remember, money cannot buy back frostbitten toes."

Q "I think that **housing off campus can be very convenient**. However, depending on the area and location where you live, the price can be outrageous for some people."

Q "Newer apartments like the University Commons and Melrose Place are becoming popular. They have pools and are run very efficiently. Always clean and such. But **you have to ride a bus just get to class**."

Q "Try to get a lot of people and split the cost of a big place. In the long run, that is **generally cheaper than a double** or even a studio."

Q "There are **tons of apartments to rent all over campus**, plus houses and townhouses. It's good."

Q "**Don't live off campus**. On campus is where to be, and there are so many options, you are bound to find something."

Q "One has to take into consideration the housing expenses (like light, heat, even cable bills). **If you want dining services, you must travel to the residence halls**. Another thing about living in apartments is their closeness to campus. Some of them are within comfortable distance to classes, but some are located in poorly-lit and poorly populated areas."

Q "If you live far away, you might find yourself tempted to drive home late at night after partying. **Not a good idea**. Save yourself the trouble and live within walking distance from the bars."

Q "Many students choose to get apartments off campus. It can be fairly inexpensive to do so, especially with roommates so that utilities are split between people. **Price does not necessarily correspond to location**, as one can find a decent apartment for $250–$300/month in the same block as a $450+/month apartment."

Q "I think that housing off campus can be very convenient. However, depending on the area and location where you live, **the price can be outrageous for some people**."

Q "Having an apartment is valuable because **the student can cook whatever she or he wants** without waiting for it to appear on the dining hall menu, and some apartment complexes allow pets, which is also important to some students."

Q "**Many students appreciate having their own room** after living in the dorm and sharing such a small living space, but others choose to continue to live in dorms because they enjoy the convenience of the dining halls and computer labs."

Q "Housing off campus is generally convenient as long as you **make a decision early**. I would say it is worth it. It is cheaper to live in an apartment than the dorms."

The College Prowler Take On...
Off-Campus Housing

Most students at U of I will tell you that off-campus housing is the only way to go. Living in the dorms for four years is just not an option for most people, not just because of the "dork" stigma, but also because it is not necessary. There are housing options all over campus, and most of them are closer to the Quad than the dorms are. This housing generally comes with a parking space and air-conditioning, both luxuries that are not included in the basic dorm package. Apartments also offer residents more space and privacy. Even if you are still sharing a room, you probably won't have to wear flip-flops in the shower or eat with 300 other people. Some people might still choose to buy a meal package, but most people are more than willing to cook their own meals for a change.

On the other hand, apartments can be costly. A single or even a double can be expensive, depending on how new the apartment is or who owns it. You might have to choose between a cheap, dilapidated apartment, or a new but expensive apartment. The only thing you should not settle for is a bad landlord. The Student Tenant Union is there for this very reason. Before you even rent an apartment, you should check with the Tenant Union to see if the apartment or landlord has had complaints filed against them. If so, you probably don't want to live there. Also, if you do end up with a bad landlord, you can go to the Union and complain. They will tell you your rights and help you with any housing questions.

A-

The College Prowler® Grade on
Off-Campus Housing: A-

A high grade in Off-Campus Housing indicates that apartments are of high quality, close to campus, affordable, and easy to secure.

Diversity

The Lowdown On...
Diversity

Native American:
0%

White:
70%

Asian American:
13%

International:
4%

African American:
7%

Out-of-State:
7%

Hispanic:
6%

Political Activity
Most of the campus is socially and politically liberal. However, these views are rarely expressed in rallies or protests, and are for the most part confined to the opinions section of the student newspaper. Not very many students are knowledgeable about the news.

Gay Pride
Groups like PFLAG and LGBT encourage tolerance, and there are SafeZones on campus. On the other hand, the gay community is not very outspoken, and it remains out of the popular culture.

Economic Status
U of I is predominantly a middle-class environment. People generally come from small or medium-sized cities throughout Illinois.

Minority Clubs
The minority clubs are active on campus. There are fraternities and sororities for different ethnicities, and the campus hosts multicultural events to encourage diversity and education.

Most Popular Religions
There are many Christian groups located on campus. Groups like Illini 4 Christ and Intervarsity are located right next to the Quad, and they are active with many believers.

Students Speak Out On...
Diversity

"The campus is very diverse. There are a lot of international students. As a whole, there are a lot of different races: white, African American, Asian American, etc."

Q "The **campus is very diverse**. Everywhere you go, you see people of different races and cultures."

Q "Oh, **we have diversity now**? Man, no one tells me anything."

Q "The campus is really diverse, and it is definitely a positive mark for our school. There are differences, but we can learn from one another and still come together for a great education. The school also hosted Culture Shock this year, and it was **a great success in promoting awareness** and having everyone work together."

Q "The campus is really diverse. **There are ethnic groups of all kinds.**"

Q "Yeah, it is definitely diverse. **I am white, and sometimes I feel like a minority.**"

Q "This campus is not really diverse. **Everyone just splits into their own cliques** and does their own thing. No one really gets together at all, that's the problem."

Q "The campus is very diverse in every way. The biggest registered student organization on campus is the Indian Students Association. **Every ethnicity, religion, and political philosophy is represented** by a student organization on campus."

Q "There are many ethnic backgrounds, but **it is mostly white here**."

Q "**It is pretty diverse**. I have never heard about a racist situation, either."

Q "From **every ethnicity, race, religion, sexual preference, ideology, and interest**, the population represents someone. The benefit of a large school is meeting a diverse group of people."

Q "As an African American female, when I came here, I did not see many brown faces, and at first, it can be a little uncomfortable. During the summer before my freshman year, I attended the orientation and the topic of discussion related to how minorities cope. **There are cultural and counseling services that are geared toward minorities** on campus, and for me, they are beneficial."

Q "Unfortunately, **there is discrimination and yes, there are hate crimes** on campus. The attacks targeting Asian American women have riled many students; the talk of affirmative action has made many people squirm in their seats, and the amount of racial slurs have gotten a lot of people very upset."

Q "There are **organizations like La Casa Cultural Latina and the African American Cultural program**, which are 'among the oldest cultural centers in the nation,' according to a U of I Web site."

Q "I think we need more international students. And no, **outside of Chicago does not mean international**."

Q "Seventy percent of the campus is made up of people from the suburbs of Chicago, but **there is a lot of diversity on campus**."

The College Prowler Take On...
Diversity

U of I is lacking in diversity. The campus is predominantly white, Christian, and middle-class. Many students would say that racism or prejudice exists here to some degree, and minorities do complain about being the only non-Caucasians in their classes. There have been targeted attacks on Asian American women and a noted increase in the use of racial slurs. Efforts are made to reach minority students, and cultural events and art shows give much needed attention to non-white students. A big debate on campus has been the issue of the Chief mascot. The campus was divided over this issue, which the NCAA recently resolved by eliminating such mascots for several colleges. Critics claimed that the practice took a sacred Native American tradition and used it for sport, while supporters claimed it was a respectful dance, a harmless tradition and a priceless institution. Currently, the University will retain the "Illini" and "Fighting Illini" nicknames. Hopefully, the change will allow former critics to feel more comfortable within the University.

Opinions on diversity really depend on the type of students you ask. A minority student will say that the campus is not diverse, but a white student will generally say the campus is very diverse. The truth is far from that. Almost 70 percent of the students are white, while there is less than 10 percent each of African Americans, Hispanics, and only 2 percent are international students. This is a discrepancy that only time can mend, and in the meantime, U of I tries to be open and accepting of all people.

The College Prowler® Grade on

Diversity: C-

A high grade in Diversity indicates that ethnic minorities and international students have a notable presence on campus and that students of different economic backgrounds, religious beliefs, and sexual preferences are well-represented.

Guys & Girls

The Lowdown On...
Guys & Girls

Men Undergrads:	Women Undergrads:
53%	47%

Birth Control Available?

Yes. McKinley Health Center offers birth control services for women who take a pelvic exam or have taken one with their previous doctor. The charge for most birth control pills is included in the health fee, which makes birth control very inexpensive and accessible for everyone. Free condoms are also handed out at McKinley and other locations.

Social Scene

As a rule, U of I students are very social and outgoing. Nearly everyone is eager to meet new people and try new things. However, people do complain that it is hard to make friends because there are a large number of people from high school who already know each other. While it is true that people may hang out with people they know at first, they do tend to separate from the old cliques after freshman year.

Hookups or Relationships?

Hookups are prevalent on campus, but relationships are also common. However, relationships are generally more relaxed and less serious, as everyone here wants to date around as much as possible. Many people come to U of I with boyfriends or girlfriends at home or elsewhere.

Best Place to Meet Guys/Girls

There are places to meet people all over campus. It is not unusual to meet people in class, as there are always topics for conversation and chances to meet up and "study." If class does not sound very romantic to you, there are people hanging out on the Quad or in the Union. These places are busy, and everyone is generally in a good mood and looking to hang out. Even though all of these locations are great for meeting people, it seems that bars and frat parties are usually where the action happens. On the weekends, nearly every bar on campus is packed with eager singles.

To ensure that people actually meet others when they are sober, U of I hosts many events for freshmen students like First Night. At these events, all of the freshmen get together for activities at the Union or in their residence halls, which always leads to new friendships and relationships. If all else fails, you can always stake out an all-girls dorm cafeteria or vice versa.

Dress Code

The dress code at U of I tends to lean toward the preppy. Most girls and guys here get ready for class, as long as it is after 9 a.m. Even when people dress down in hoodies and jeans, they tend to wear Aeropostale hoodies or Abercrombie jeans. However, just because the mainstream dresses that way does not mean everyone does. A lot of people here choose to find their own niche, whether it be in the form of purple high tops or vintage clothing. Don't worry about going along with the crowd too much. People may care about their appearance here, but that does not mean they care about anyone else's.

Did You Know?

Top Places to Find Hotties:
1. The Union
2. The Quad
3. The bars

Top Places to Hook Up:
1. Frat parties
2. Dorm rooms
3. Shadowy bar corners
4. Parking lots
5. Apartment parties

Guys & Girls

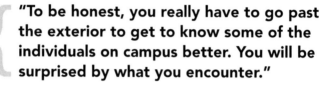

"To be honest, you really have to go past the exterior to get to know some of the individuals on campus better. You will be surprised by what you encounter."

Q "Because it's a large campus, there are **a lot of good-looking guys**. Unfortunately, they tend to be aware of their looks. There are a lot of different kinds of guys depending on your type."

Q **"Well, I am pretty good looking**. Seriously. Come to school here and you can see for yourself."

Q "Girls here are too obsessed with getting a guy. It is so 1950s. They all get dolled up for class and run around in tube tops in the winter. No wonder **McKinley is always running out of free condoms**."

Q "The guys here are fratty. **They all wear Greek stuff and are too preppy**. I wish I could take their hair gel away from them, just for a day. They would probably kill themselves."

Q "Most of the hot girls on campus can be found in the sorority houses, which is good because they travel in packs. **The hook-up culture is very prevalent** on our campus due to the insane amounts of alcohol we consume. The trends of girls' clothes usually take on monumental proportions where you can literally see 40 or 50 girls wearing the same thing in one night (which wasn't so bad when the half shirt thing came along)."

Q "Oh, geez . . . I bet all the guys are telling you how hot they are and how the girls need to work out or something. This is a stupid question. **Who comes to college to meet hot people**? This isn't *Boy Meets World*."

Q "There are **not a lot of hot guys**. There are some mediocre guys. Medicore isn't hot."

Q "Basically, **most sorority girls like fraternity guys** and everything else just depends on what night it is and how much everybody has had to drink. The hottest houses on campus are the SDTs, Chi Omegas, and the DGs."

Q "Well, for the most part, **all of the guys are alive and breathing**. That is always good. Other than that, well, yeah they are alive."

Q "Girls here are out of control. It is the sorority thing. **Sexy women, yeah**."

Q "**'Hooking up' and 'shacking' are terms not altogether foreign to most UIUC ears**, but McKinley Health Center provides free condoms and birth control to help keep students informed and responsible about their dating decisions."

Q "Yeah, **we are a good looking campus**. After all, this is where Hugh Hefner first learned to appreciate beautiful women."

Q "Like parties, **no two boys are the same**. Of course you will run into the familiar labels like: 'the frat boys,' 'the engineering boys,' 'the PAR boys,' or those 'Kappa boys.'"

Q "Sometimes **girls just wear sweats to class**. But hey, that's still cool with me."

Q "It is **a veritable buffet of men**. Seriously, girls, take your pick."

Q "The **girls here are A plus**. The blonds here are choice. All the sororities here . . . they make for beautiful women."

The College Prowler Take On...
Guys & Girls

U of I is home to many different types of people, but for the most part, the mainstream seems concerned with their appearance and social life. Students here place a high value on what they do on the weekends and who they are dating, so in a lot of ways, it can feel like high school instead of college. This is especially true of the bar scene. Not many people go out at night in T-shirts and sneakers. Most people get dressed up, especially on the weekends. Typical social wear for a guy includes a button-down long sleeve shirt with vintage jeans and some kind of necklace, while girls wear mini-skirts, black pants, dark jeans, and some kind of low or tight top. Even in the dead of winter, you will still see girls in nothing but a tube top and a mini, which should give you some idea of how important appearances are here.

As far as looks, most people find that the girls here are very attractive, so much so that they think Hugh Hefner would feel the same way, too. In general, students seem certain that it's possible to find someone you're attracted to for either a hookup or a relationship.

The College Prowler® Grade on
Guys: A-

A high grade for Guys indicates that the male population on campus is attractive, smart, friendly, and engaging, and that the school has a decent ratio of guys to girls.

The College Prowler® Grade on
Girls: A-

A high grade for Girls not only implies that the women on campus are attractive, smart, friendly, and engaging, but also that there is a fair ratio of girls to guys.

Athletics

The Lowdown On...
Athletics

Athletic Division:
Division I-A

Conference:
Big Ten

Males Playing Varsity Sports:
327 (2%)

Females Playing Varsity Sports:
222 (2%)

Men's Varsity Sports:

Baseball
Basketball
Cheerleading
Cross Country
Football
Golf
Gymnastics
Tennis
Track/Field
Wrestling

Women's Varsity Sports:

Basketball
Cheerleading
Cross Country
Golf
Gymnastics
Soccer
Softball
Swimming/Diving
Tennis
Track/Field
Volleyball

Club Sports:

Badminton
Bowling
Climbing
Cricket
Dance
Fencing
Figure Skating
Hockey
Ju Jitsu
Lacrosse
Racquetball
Rugby
Synchronized Ice Skating
Underwater Hockey
Water Polo
Water Skiing
Weightlifting

Intramurals:

Broomball
Dodgeball
Flag Football
Mini Golf
NCAA Basketball Pick 'em
Sand Volleyball
Softball
Tennis
Ultimate Frisbee
Volleyball
Wiffleball

School Mascot

Fighting Illini

Athletic Fields

Armory, Assembly Hall, Atkins Outdoor Courts, Complex Fields, CRCE (Wimpe), Eichelberger Field, Florida and Lincoln Playing Fields, Freer Hall, Ice Arena, Illini Grove, Illinois Field, IMPE, Irwin Indoor Football Practice Facility, Kenney Gym, Memorial Stadium, Multiplex Playing Fields, Ubenn Basketball Facility

Best Place to Take a Walk

Allerton Park, Arboretum, or Japan House Gardens

Getting Tickets

It is usually easy to get tickets for sporting events, as long as it is not a big game. There is generally a good turnout, especially at the football and basketball games. Money is not an issue either, as you can get a good price with your student ID.

Most Popular Sports

There is a lot of interest in sports, especially football and basketball. The fate of these two teams is taken personally by students and community residents alike, and everyone goes to the games to support them and cheer them on, regardless of the weather.

Overlooked Teams

The women's tennis team has done very well in the past, however, the women tend to get overshadowed by the men's tennis team.

Gyms/Facilities

IMPE

IMPE is the main gym on campus. It is home to four different gyms as well as a variety of sports fields. There are tennis courts, squash courts, racquetball courts, wallyball courts, volleyball courts, and a free weight room. It also has two pools, a sauna, and an indoor running track. This is a favorite hangout of many students, which unfortunately means it can get busy. IMPE is currently being remodeled, which will be good in the long run, but in the meantime, it means extra annoyance and lack of space.

Wimpe (CRCE)

Wimpe is a smaller gym, located right next door to Allen Hall and Lincoln Avenue Residence Halls, which is very convenient for its residents. Unfortunately, this also means that it is very busy, and it is rarely empty, no matter what the time.

Playing Fields

All of the playing fields are well-kept and lit for playing at night.

Students Speak Out On...
Athletics

"University of Illinois is a Division I Big Ten contender in every sport. If nothing else, the weekend is always filled with sporting events to watch—football and basketball particularly, but it extends to every sport."

Q "Varsity sports are pretty big, but **fans tend to be fair-weather fans**. Intramural sports are pretty big."

Q "Varsity sports on campus are pretty big. **We were the Big Ten champs** for basketball, and our other teams such as tennis and volleyball are also very good. The IM sports are pretty good and easy to get involved in from broomball to volleyball and softball."

Q "Sports are important on campus whether you participate or not. **I do not really follow sports myself,** though."

Q "**Football and basketball are big** here. They are a major topic on this campus."

Q "Varsity is big, but so are campus sports. I been involved in a few leagues—most people are. There is **a big variety of IM sports**."

Q "A recent NCAA Tennis champion is from U of I. **Intramural sports are very big** as well. From basketball to soccer, during every season of the year, there is always an intramural sport offered."

Q "Sports suck! But yeah, they are everywhere. You have to go to games. Literally, **people drag you there and stick a foam finger on your hand**. Don't come here if you are allergic to foam fingers."

Q "We are a big ten college. 'Nuf said. U of I has had some of the best men's basketball and football teams in the nation. Like other Big Ten colleges, **we have our ups and downs**. But that does not keep students from flocking towards the games, or parents and visitors coming from all over Illinois as well."

Q "If you are a sports fan, invest in those season tickets early. If you like Dee Brown and like going to every single basketball game (like some people I know), there is this club called Orange Crush where you and the team can benefit from student participation. **The women's volleyball team, I hear, is really exceptional as well**."

Q "At a Big Ten University, basketball and football rule. In the last four years, **we boasted two bowl game appearances** and a Big Ten Championship under head coach Ron Turner, as well as three Big Ten Championships and four bids to the NCAA Tournament losing only to Kansas (twice), Arizona, and Notre Dame."

Q "I am not really sure about IM sports. I don't hear much about them. As for varsity, **football and basketball are big around here**."

Q "**Illinois consistently puts eight to ten athletes in the pros every year**. Former Illinis Jameel Cook, Simeon Rice, and Ken Dilger won a Super Bowl with the Buccaneers. 2003 saw cornerback Eugene Wilson picked 35th overall, and in 2002 Frank Williams was a first round pick for the New York Knicks. The tennis team won the national title in 2003 as well."

Q "Varsity sports are a force to be reckoned with here. It seems that **everyone gets real excited about one sport or another**. There'll be talk such as, 'Man, did you see the girls' volleyball last night,' or 'I didn't know our wrestling team was seventh in the nation.'"

Q "The student fan group on campus, Illini Pride, is one of the largest of its kind in the nation and there is a **never a dull moment** in sports here in Urbana-Champaign."

Q "From intramural broomball on the ice to dodgeball, there isn't really a whole lot missing. **Flag football under the lights in the fall** is when all the high school all-stars get to relive their past glories (trust me, I know from experience here). There is something for everyone, whether you want to watch or play, we have a lot of flat land on which to do either."

The College Prowler Take On...
Athletics

Athletics at U of I are big, and people take sports very seriously. Whether they are spectators or participants in the game, nearly everyone on campus is interested in the outcome of the varsity sports teams. As far as basketball and football are concerned, you'll find more students buzzing over and attending those games than you will any other sport on campus. But this is a Division I school, so that's expected. Intramural and club sports are also really big on campus, and the underwater hockey team is legendary for its crazy games. Even if you are not the best athlete you can surely find some sport that interests you, like dodge ball. You might not get a scholarship for it, though. Intramural sports are a good way to meet people and have fun.

The gyms and playing fields are also big on campus, and most people say that they consider IMPE one of their favorite hangouts. Of course, the real event here is football. People come to the games religiously, rain or snow. The Block I section is for the most dedicated of fans. There, students dress in all orange and blue and hold signs to cheer on their team. The Illinettes also turn out for all the home games, and so it's like a midday party. Even people that are not that interested in football come out for the party atmosphere and school spirit. So if you're not a sports fan when you come to U of I, don't be surprised if you graduate with a foam finger on your hand.

A-

The College Prowler® Grade on
Athletics: A-

A high grade in Athletics indicates that students have school spirit, that sports programs are respected, that games are well-attended, and that intramurals are a prominent part of student life.

Nightlife

The Lowdown On...
Nightlife

Club and Bar Prowler: Popular Nightlife Spots!

Club Crawler:

The clubs at U of I are only moderately popular, possibly because they have a stricter dress code and check IDs more carefully at the door. Still, they have really good live music and special events.

Canopy Club
708 S. Goodwin Avenue
(217) 367-3140

The Canopy Club is host to live music almost every day of the week. Ages 19-and-up—and they do not joke around about IDs. They also have 15 different beers on tap. If you are looking for a good place to hear music and chill, this is the place for you.

Cowboy Monkey

6 Taylor Street

(217) 398-2688

Cowboy Monkey is a restaurant/club. There is live music almost every night, and the cover is generally never more than five dollars. Ages 19-and-up, and IDs are checked. Cowboy Monkey caters to an older crowd and you won't generally find many freshmen here. However, they do have good live music, ranging from rock to reggae to hip-hop. Metered parking.

Elmer's Club 45

3525 N. Cunningham Avenue

(217) 344-3101

Elmer's is host to live music and dancing. It is not as close to campus as other bars, but it's still fun. However, it is generally not popular with the younger and more mainstream set.

Highdive

51 Main Street

(217) 356-2337

The Highdive is one of the most popular off-campus bars. Minimum age is 19-and-up, and they do check IDs carefully. There is a dress code, which prohibits hats or doo-rags for men. You can park at the nearby meters for no charge, but you might have to walk a little bit.

(Highdive, continued)

There is a huge dance floor and they generally host a variety of live music. There is a DJ every Friday and Saturday night. The cover ranges from five to ten dollars depending on the event.

Tonic

619 S. Wright Street

(847) 331-6272

Tonic is an on-campus club that is next to Green Street. It is two floors, the bottom is for dancing, and the top is for lounging and drinking. The music leans towards techno, although there is also hip-hop. This club is for a young, hip crowd, but they do check IDs to make sure you are 19-and-up. This is more of a dressy club, and although they do not have a strict dress code, you should try to dress nice.

Specials: On certain nights (such as after breaks), Tonic hosts back to school events in which you can buy a $5 wristband that provides an open bar and free cover for a couple of hours.

Bar Prowler:

The bars at U of I are very popular. Although people do get dressed up to go out, it is acceptable to come in jeans and a T-shirt. Most are located on campus, and so they are generally in walking distance or on the bus line.

Barfly

120 N. Neil Street

(217) 352-9756

The Barfly has a large beer garden and inside lounge. There is also generally a DJ. Not a hot bar with the younger crowd, Barfly is still fun and popular. They generally play hip-hop music. Barfly is definitely a good place to check out.

Clybourne

708 S. Sixth Street

(217) 383-1008

Clybourne is legendary on campus for its Tuesday Wine Night. Nearly everyone that goes out on Tuesday inevitably stops by Clybourne for a bottle of wine. However, even though it does stay busy on the weekends, it is not one of the popular dance spots. There is no dance floor and is more of a bar/grill. They still have a DJ though, and some nights the line goes all the way out the door. Age requirement is 19-and-up and IDs are not checked too hard; but you may have to wait to get in, especially if it is Wine Night.

C.O. Daniels

608 E. Daniel Street

(217) 337-7411

C.O. Daniels is a smaller bar, with only one big room and little dance space. In fact, only a few people dance here, and instead it is more of a hangout. There is a mechanical bull there and contests are common. The cover is generally inexpensive, but it is also not as popular as the other bars, so there are not as many people. 19-and-up and IDs are checked moderately hard.

Gully's

306 E. Green Street

(217) 384-0500

Gully's is a great campus bar. It does have a "Greek bar" reputation, and some GDIs claim to feel uncomfortable there. But even if you are not Greek, ignore the naysayers, because this is a great place to chill and dance.

Iron Post

120 S. Race

(217) 337-7678

The Iron Post is located in Downtown Urbana and it is not very popular with most University students. It is more of a community bar, and thus you won't find many students hanging out there.

(Iron Post, continued)

However, they do offer live music a few times a week, ranging from jazz to acoustic, and the atmosphere is friendly and inviting. But don't look for a smoke machine and disco lights here.

It's Brothers Bar and Grill

613 E. Green Street

(217) 328-5531

It's Brothers is a popular campus bar. 19-and-up, but they do not joke around about underage drinking here. They do serve great wings and people often stop by just for that. It's Brothers is one of the few bars on campus that is popular with all of the students and yet still never too crowded or too crazy. You might not even get a beer spilled on you, which makes it much safer than some of the other campus bars. Underage kids complain that the atmosphere is a little hostile. But, then again, can you blame them for not serving alcohol to minors?

Specials: Saturdays: Pucker Night, Wednesdays: Mug Club, Mondays: Pitcher Night

Joe's Brewery

706 S. Fifth Street

(217) 384-1790

Joe's Brewery is really two bars in one. The front rooms are very laid-back with pool tables and lounges. Joe's has three floors, but most of the action happens on the main level. The back room is darker and used almost exclusively as a dance floor. 19-and-up and IDs are checked moderately hard. There are usually a wide variety of ages and people here, and the music ranges from techno to hip-hop. There is generally a DJ on the weekends.

Kam's

618 E. Daniel Street

(217) 337-3300

Kam's is one of the most popular bars on campus, and it is also one of the most laid-back. Kam's has two floors, a beer garden, and a dance floor. It is almost always packed on the weekends. The age is 19-and-up, but Kam's is known to be easy on fake IDs and underage kids. However, things are tightening up. Kam's is host to events like "CatFights" and they generally have MTV celebrities from *Real World* and *Road Rules* stop by throughout the year. Also, a karaoke machine makes appearances.

Legends

522 E. Green Street

(217) 355-7674

Located right in the heart of Green Street, Legends is one of the more popular campus bars. There is a beer garden and an inside area with pool tables where you can lounge. Age limit is 19-and-up and IDs are checked very hard here. This is not much of a place to dance, although people do occasionally. This is more of a place to chill after class and beyond.

Murphy's Pub

604 E. Green Street

(217) 352-7275

Murphy's is popular with the older crowd, primarily because it offers a peaceful and easygoing atmosphere. There are darts, pool tables, and a jukebox that allows you to choose your own music. However, not much dancing goes on, as people prefer to sit and chill with their friends. You can also get a meal until 10 p.m. So if you want to avoid the insanity that inevitably comes with dance clubs and Justin Timberlake music, check out Murphy's. And no matter the day, Murphy's never charges cover.

Rose Bowl Tavern

106 N. Race Street

(217) 367-7031

Rose Bowl is host to frequent live music, typically country.

(Rose Bowl Tavern, continued)

It is a fun place to escape the never ending hip-hop club music, not to mention the bands are awesome. It is one of the few excellent country music bars in the area.

Station 211

211 E. Green Street

(217) 367-9915

Station 211 is a favorite hangout of the young and single crowd. It is also becoming known as a "Greek" bar. Situated on one floor with an adjoining beer garden, it resembles a medieval castle on the outside. But the inside is purely contemporary, with one huge bar and a floor for dancing. Actually, there is no real dance floor, but that has never stopped anyone in the past. People love coming here after games or class, and it is just as popular at night. 19-and-up, and word is that IDs are checked super hard here.

White Horse

112½ E. Green Street

(217) 352-5945

White Horse is a popular spot where young people like to sit and hang out. Bars used for just hanging out are generally only for the older crowd, but many young people enjoy White Horse. It is moderately busy throughout the weekend. You must be 19-and-up and IDs are checked fairly hard.

Student Favorites:

Kam's

Station 211

Highdive

Murphy's Pub

Bars Close At:

2 a.m.

Useful Resources for Nightlife:

Buzz magazine

C-U CitiView

Daily Illini newspaper

www.cucalendar.com

Primary Areas with Nightlife:

Green Street

Daniel Street

Wright Street

Downtown Champaign

Cheapest Place to Get a Drink:

Kam's

Local Specialties:

Captain and Coke, Jagermeister, Car Bomb, Boone's, Miller Lite

Other Places to Check Out

The Union usually hosts non-alcoholic events that involve everything from dancing to palm reading. It is a good place to escape the drinking that can sometimes take over campus.

What to Do if You're Not 21

If you are not 21, you can still have fun at U of I. If you are looking for a bar/club atmosphere, most are 19-and-up. Frat parties are always popular, as are apartment parties. If you are looking to escape the drinking scene, there is always something happening.

Nightlife

> "Usually the most popular fraternities on campus throw 'after hours' from whenever everybody clears out of the bars (which close at 1 a.m.) until whenever. On average they consist of a DJ and beer."

Q "U of I definitely has **a big bar atmosphere**. There are always frat and apartment parties to go to. My favorite bars are probably Kam's and Station 211."

Q "There is a lot to do, but it usually involves parties and bars. **Not much else goes on here.**"

Q "Whatever people are doing, I guess that is where the party is. **Brothers and Murphy's are always good**. There is stuff happening every night."

Q "**Frats are the places for parties**. I don't really have any favorites though. I just follow the crowd."

Q "**House parties are not as popular at the University as at other campuses**, although they are great once you have a group of friends and don't feel like worrying about police bar raids (which only happen in campus bars) or getting into fraternity parties. House and apartment parties usually are not publicized across campus, and are usually only open to friends of those throwing the party."

Q "**The bars are all chill**. Brothers is the best, though. You can just hang there with your friends."

Q "Check out on-campus bars Legends and Murphy's Pub if you want a low-key night of drinking beer with friends. If you feel like dancing but want to stay on campus, head to Tonic. **Stay away from Station and Gully's,** two campus bars, unless you are in the Greek system. Off campus, check out Cowboy Monkey and the Highdive for great live music and fun—though very smoky—atmospheres."

Q "It is on Green Street where many of the bars, like Brothers and Kam's, are located. **Green Street is the location that many of the parties take place.** Private housing, like Bromley and Illini Towers, both on campus, boast many parties as well. Off campus, the choices are more generally private parties."

Q "Most parties on campus are referred to as pre-games, or after hours, due to the fact that everything revolves around the campus bars. **There are a lot of house parties at the beginning of the year** because of Greek dry rush, but after that, it's all about the after hours."

Q "**Bars, bars, and more bars.** When you come to the University of Illinois, you will most likely be introduced early on to the various bars on and off campus. And you won't have to wait until you are of legal age to drink, either; you can get into Champaign bars after your 19th birthday, and in Urbana bars, you are good to go once you turn 18 years old."

Q "The best houses to post-party at are ZBT, Pikes, Sigma Chi, and Sammie's. One of the most infamous parties of the year is thrown late March or early April. AEPi has the distinction of the Watermelon Slush. **Thousands of carved watermelons filled with jungle juice,** about ten thousand Jello shots, more beer than *Animal House,* and great live bands makes this one of the highlights of second semester."

Q "The bar scene is an unbreakable tradition at the University. The two longest standing bars with the most school spirit would definitely be Joe's and Kam's which have their walls lined with pictures of the greatest athletes ever to have played there. If you want to get to a bar where you can experience sorority girls up close, go to Gully's. **Murphy's is like St. Patrick's Day all year long**, where they have a clock that counts down to the famous Irish drinking holiday."

Q "The place to see and be seen by all is definitely Station 211; it's big and cozy all at the same time, and it sports **the best beer garden on campus**."

Q "**Bars and alcohol are so big around here**, sometimes you think that is all there is. It's sad sometimes, because you look back and can't remember most of the nights you had with your friends. Now that I am graduating, I wish I had spent more time sober and trying new things. Not new drinks, new things."

Q "Kam's is the big chill bar here. Sometimes they are a little too trashy, though. **The place is really gross**, and people fight a lot."

Q "**Pre-drink, drink, after drinks**. It is all about bars here. Screw clubs. Try Brothers or maybe Joe's on a good night. Don't wait in line for anywhere but Highdive. Never wait for Station. Kam's, maybe, if the line goes fast. Never, ever, ever waste time waiting for C.O.'s."

The College Prowler Take On...
Nightlife

Nightlife is very popular. The bar and club scene is crowded every weekend, and they tend to be just as busy during the week. Specials like Tuesday Wine Night tell you that the party gets started early around here. Closing time was recently extended to 2 a.m. in some locations, which has definitely made some party animals, who hate to go home, happy. Parties here do not start or end in bars for most students. There is generally something called pre-dinking or pre-gaming in which students begin drinking in their dorms or apartments. (But remember, the dorms are alcohol free, and we do not encourage you to be stupid. Still, it happens.) Once the bars close, everyone pours out to either an after-party at a frat or an apartment.

When choosing a bar or club, you just need to feel a few places out. Even those that cater to a young crowd do not always appeal to younger students, and those that cater to an older crowd do not always appeal to older students. If you want to dance, go to a place that has a dance floor, but if you want to chill and just hear some good live music, then avoid places that only play hip-hop for the dancing crowd. U of I has so many options that you are sure to find a half a dozen places that you love, although some complain that campus bars are overrun by the teeny bopper scene. If you are looking to avoid the bar scene, there are certainly things to do on campus. You can always catch a show at Krannert, a game at the Union, or a concert at Assembly Hall.

A-

The College Prowler® Grade on
Nightlife: A-

A high grade in Nightlife indicates that there are many bars and clubs in the area that are easily accessible and affordable. Other determining factors include the number of options for the under-21 crowd and the prevalence of house parties.

Greek Life

The Lowdown On...
Greek Life

Number of Fraternities:
46

Number of Sororities:
23

Undergrad Men in Fraternities:
20%

Undergrad Women in Sororities:
22%

Fraternities on Campus:

Acacia
Alpha Chi Rho
Alpha Delta Phi
Alpha Epsilon Pi
Alpha Gamma Rho
Alpha Gamma Sigma
Alpha Kappa Lambda
Alpha Sigma Phi
Alpha Tau Omega
Beta Sigma Psi
Beta Theta Pi
Chi Psi
Delta Chi
Delta Phi
Delta Sigma Phi
Delta Tau Delta
Delta Upsilon
Farmhouse
Kappa Delta Rho
Kappa Sigma
Lambda Chi Alpha
Omega Delta
Omega Delta Phi
Phi Delta Theta
Phi Gamma Delta Colony
Phi Kappa Psi
Phi Kappa Sigma
Phi Sigma Kappa
Pi Kappa Alpha
Pi Kappa Phi
Pi Lambda Phi
Psi Upsilon
Sigma Alpha Mu
Sigma Chi
Sigma Nu

(Fraternities, continued)

Sigma Phi Delta
Sigma Phi Epsilon
Sigma Pi
Sigma Tau Gamma
Tau Epsilon Phi
Tau Kappa Epsilon
Theta Chi
Theta Xi
Triangle
Zeta Beta Tau
Zeta Psi

Sororities on Campus:

4-H House
Alpha Chi Omega
Alpha Delta Pi
Alpha Epsilon Phi
Alpha Gamma Delta
Alpha Omega Epsilon
Alpha Omicron Pi
Alpha Phi
Chi Omega
Delta Delta Delta
Delta Gamma
Delta Xi Phi
Delta Zeta
Gamma Phi Beta
Kappa Alpha Theta
Kappa Delta
Kappa Kappa Gamma
Phi Mu
Phi Sigma Sigma
Pi Beta Phi
Sigma Alpha
Sigma Delta Tau
Sigma Kappa

Multicultural Colonies:

Alpha Phi Alpha
Alpha Kappa Alpha
Beta Phi Phi
Delta Sigma Theta
Iota Phi Theta
Kappa Alpha Psi
Omega Psi Phi
Phi Beta Sigma
Phi Rho Eta
Sigma Gamma Rho
Zeta Phi Beta

Other Greek Organizations:

Greek Council
Greek Peer Advisors
Interfraternity Council
National Panhellenic Council
Order of Omega
Panhellenic Council

Did You Know?

The University of Illinois is among the top schools in the country in terms of **pure volume of Greek organizations**.

Students Speak Out On...
Greek Life

> "Greek letters symbolize more than partying; they can be beneficial to your academic life. U of I has such a large Greek system that you can find organizations that cater to your academic field."

Q "There are a lot of Greeks here. I mean, **I am not involved, but I know plenty of people who are**. Not everybody, though."

Q "**Greek isn't my thing**. You basically have to choose: Christian or Greek. But it does not dominate too much. Do your own thing, no problem."

Q "Greeks definitely dominate the social scene. If I remember right, **we have the largest Greek system in the country**."

Q "There are **so many Greeks here**! But I'm not. So there."

Q "There is opportunity for anyone who wants to be part of the system to join during Rush Week. However, **one can live a perfectly happy life without being Greek**. They might have to pay a bit more to get into the parties, though."

Q "I have not pledged yet, but I can't wait until fall semester when I can. **The Greek experience can be fun but tedious** because there are a lot of decisions involved, like rush and pledging. Hopefully, all the work and uncertainty is worthwhile."

Q "Greek life is great. **It is so easy to find a house that fits you**."

Q "There are so many other things to do here that **I almost wish that I hadn't joined a house**."

Q "**Greek life is so ridiculous**. A group of people who get together and make people pay to be their friends— seriously, it is the 'in crowd' at its most arrogant and excessive. Screw them and do your own thing."

Q "Interestingly enough, a social scene exists outside of fraternities and sororities. From the bars to apartments to house parties, lots of other stuff happens, but when it comes down to it, **Greeks are everywhere**."

Q "As a whole, the Greek system makes this campus what it is. For better or worse, **we are proud to be who we are**. And the best part about having such a huge percentage of Greeks is that participation is not relegated to a certain kind of person, but instead, there is a house or an organization for everyone."

Q "I do not belong to a sorority, but I cannot go to class, to a bar, a restaurant, or even walk down the street without seeing a student with letters on his or her jacket, shirt, or hat. **Greek organizations are prominent on campus**, but at the same time, not being in one doesn't put me at a disadvantage."

Q "If you choose to join the Greek system at Illinois, **you will not be short on choices**. Some are known as being mean and others as sweet, some as heavy partiers and others as prudes, some as urban and others as rural. But regardless of what house you join, expect at least a little stereotyping and a little pressure to conform to those in your house."

Q "**Partying does play a big part in the Greek social scene**, and certain bars have become unofficially 'Greek' bars where generally only people in Greek houses go."

Q "Regardless of whether you join the system, the main drawback to having such a large Greek community on such an already large and clique-oriented campus is that Greeks and non-Greeks generally do not interact socially. **The two scenes remain largely separate**, and who knows whether that will ever change."

The College Prowler Take On...
Greek Life

This campus is really into Greek life. Everywhere you go, you see frat houses and sorority houses, and you can't go outside without running into someone with their letters. For people who want to go Greek, this is good news, as it gives them so many options to choose from. For those who are hesitant about joining a frat or sorority, it may feel overwhelming, because it seems like everyone is in a house but you. In fact, one of the first questions most people will ask you is, "Are you in a house?" This does not mean that everyone is Greek. In fact, a large percentage of undergraduates are not, but it is still a very powerful force on campus. On Quad Day, these organizations spill out on the campus, searching for new recruits who want to rush.

However, there are also other clubs and groups that come out on Quad Day. Don't feel that you have to join the Greek system just to make friends, because nothing could be further from the truth. In fact, some people say that Greeks have fewer friends because they never try to meet people outside of their house. If you are into partying, you should know that having one of the biggest Greek systems in the country means more events and more craziness. On the other hand, you should also know that it means the campus can sometimes feel cliqueish when you first arrive. However, once you get to know people and find your niche, you will see that both Greeks and independents get along very well and have few conflicts.

The College Prowler® Grade on

Greek Life: A+

A high grade in Greek Life indicates that sororities and fraternities are not only present, but also active on campus. Other determining factors include the variety of houses available and the respect the Greek community receives from the rest of the campus.

Drug Scene

The Lowdown On...
Drug Scene

Most Prevalent Drugs on Campus:
Alcohol
Cocaine
Marijuana
LSD

Liquor-Related Referrals:
328

Liquor-Related Arrests:
374

Drug-Related Referrals:
67

Drug-Related Arrests:
79

Drug Counseling Programs

Alcohol and Other Drug Office (AODO)

(217) 333-7757

Services: AODO assessment and evaluation, group therapy, individual counseling, Challenging Alcohol Attitudes Positively (CAAP) classes, marijuana information classes, referrals/options to other area groups

Alcohol and Drug Services at Counseling Center

(217) 333-3704

Services: Assessment, counseling, outreach and consultation,intervention, referral

Dial-A-Nurse

Phone: (217) 333-2700

Faculty/Staff Assistance Program

(217) 244-5312

Services: Confidential assessment, referral, and community program information

L.W's Place

(217) 356-4600

Services: Assessment, therapy

Prairie Center for Substance Abuse

(217) 328-4500

Services: Assessment, therapy

The Pavilion

(217) 373-1700

Services: Assessment, therapy

Students Speak Out On...
Drug Scene

"The drug scene is pretty typical at the University of Illinois. There is a zero-tolerance policy in the dorms. If one has the desire to get drugs or alcohol illegally, it is possible."

Q "Drugs are average here. It is **mostly like the high school drug scene**. Of course, everyone drinks."

Q "The drug scene is definitely there—with people of this age, it is always going to be there. But **it is nothing that gets out of hand**."

Q "I have no knowledge on the drug scene. I guess **it is under control**."

Q "Beyond liquor, **there does not seem to be a major problem with substance abuse** on campus. Seriously, I think that you will find something if you search for it."

Q "One word describes the general drug scene on campus: pot. There is lots and lots of marijuana. Your neighbor probably smokes. It's not just potheads, either. People smoke-up to write papers, do engineering homework, to study, to go out, to play Frisbee. **Everybody is smoking, and everybody is selling**."

Q "Cocaine is starting to make a small resurgence as a high-class party drug, but people are becoming aware of how dangerous it is. The ecstasy craze is dying from what it was a couple of years ago. **The number one experimental drug right now is mushrooms**. The second most popular drug to marijuana is nitrous . . . go figure."

Q "Well, when I was living in the dorms, **there were some people caught smoking marijuana**, and they were dealt with by residence hall authorities. I am not really sure what the punishment was."

Q "Well, I have been offered pot and acid. **I have heard rumors of coke**, and I know some people take cold and pain medicine to get more of a buzz when drinking. But most people just stick to beer. Hell, it's cheaper."

Q "**The biggest drug is Metabolife**. Seriously, all the sorority chicks are scarfing those things with their Diet Cokes day and night."

Q "Drugs are **not a problem**."

Q "What was the question? Just joking. Drugs are limited and not worth it. **Most people don't bother**. This is not high school, you know. Pot isn't that cool anymore."

The College Prowler Take On...
Drug Scene

The drug scene at U of I is limited to acid and pot for casual users, and even then, usage of these drugs is generally not very popular or extreme. These drugs are available, though, as most students say they either know of someone who has gotten drugs or someone who supplies drugs. Instead, alcohol is the substance of choice, and many students do abuse it. It is not uncommon to find students who drink four or five times a week. As a consequence, most substance abuse arrests are related to alcohol and range from fights to underage drinking to driving while under the influence. Occurences of violence, both physical and sexual, that are caused by alcohol are probably some of the larger problems caused by substance abuse on this campus. U of I tries to educate its students on these dangers, and it even requires all freshmen to take a class on rape drugs and ways to stay safe while around alcohol.

Of course, no matter how many seminars U of I sponsors, there will always be some students who have a problem with control and safety. The best thing you can do is avoid people and places that are dangerous and far from campus. Even if you and your friends head out for what you intend to be an innocent night on the town, you never know what can go on at a party once you get there. Champaign tends to be a harder scene, with more drugs present and available, especially in the seedier part of town. Practice self-control and safety around alcohol, and the rest should not be a problem.

B-

The College Prowler® Grade on

Drug Scene: B-

A high grade in the Drug Scene indicates that drugs are not a noticeable part of campus life; drug use is not visible, and no pressure to use them seems to exist.

Campus Strictness

The Lowdown On...
Campus Strictness

What Are You Most Likely to Get Caught Doing on Campus:

- Drinking underage
- Fighting
- Speeding
- Turning right on a red light
- Illegal substances in the dorms
- Pulling fire alarms
- Illegal parking
- Cheating
- Jaywalking
- Theft
- Not stopping for pedestrians

Students Speak Out On...
Campus Strictness

> "Campus police are ever-present on the University of Illinois campus, but if you're safe walking down the street with a beer it's up to chance—whether you will get away with it depends on the night."

Q "Depending on the situation, **the police can be strict**. Like fake IDs—they really crack down on them."

Q "I have known people—good student types—who have gotten anything from drinking tickets to arrested. My best advice is be nice to cops. **They can screw you over if they want to**."

Q "Since 18- and 19-year-olds can get into bars in Urbana-Champaign, cops tend to be fairly lax on policing house, apartment, and fraternity parties. **Frat parties rarely get into trouble**, and house and apartment parties usually only have trouble when the police receive complaints from neighbors. Watch out for police bar raids, which are usually spread by word-of-mouth beforehand."

Q "In Urbana-Champaign, a person only has to be 19 to get into a bar. Therefore, almost everyone at the University can get into the bars, although they are technically not allowed to drink. So the **campus police are pretty harsh if they catch a person**. Expect a $200 fine if a person is drinking before they are 21, and he or she is caught."

Q "Yeah, **I hear about busts now and then**. Personally, I wouldn't know because I don't go out to bars too much."

Q "A law was passed about a year ago under which anyone convicted of underage drinking **can lose her or his license** for up to a year, and the increased security in the bars reflects this change in legislature."

Q "It's a given that **you can get alcoholic drinks in a bar, regardless of your age**. Underage students can easily find of-age people to get them drinks, but be careful because getting caught with a drink in your hand costs you upwards of $250 in drinking fines."

Q "**The cops are out there**, sure. But as long as you conceal what you are doing—and you would be stupid not to—you should be fine."

Q "When you put alcohol and Urbana-Champaign in the same sentence, you get campus police and angry parents. It is strongly recommended that to be on the safe side: **do not drink if you are under 21**. You can run, but you cannot hide from them."

Q "Campus police are so so strict when it comes to underage drinking that even if a person under the age of 21 is sitting within arm's length of a bottle of Budweiser, they will get reprimanded and ticketed. **They do not play around**."

Q "**They have been said to go undercover**, like they were college students trying to have a good time, laughing in your face, but then will snap you up within the next second."

Q "In the dorms, and depending on your RA, underage drinking is forbidden. If you are of age, then **you should not have a problem** (unless you're clowning at 3 a.m. in the morning)."

Q "I think that for the most part **the police can't get a finger into the drug scene**. Mostly because people keep it in its place because they are more careful not to get caught."

Q "The police really crack down on underage drinking and alcohol related offenses. Everything from public intoxication to open containers and DUIs carry heavy fines. **Noise violations are usually hit pretty hard**, too."

Q "Recently, there has been more attention paid to underage drinking, and federal funding was granted for state police officers to assist the local police in catching underage drinkers at bars. **Plain clothes officers come to the bars occasionally**."

The College Prowler Take On...
Campus Strictness

U of I is relatively tough on its students, although, as one student said, it really depends on the situation you find yourself in. The campus police do not turn a blind eye to drunks, and never to students caught drinking underage. They are also tough on drugs and fights, especially when those fights take place in a bar. Police bar raids are not uncommon, and some students say that there are times when raids can be predicted. Situations that involve alcohol and narcotics can really get out of control, which is why cops aren't easy on offenders. Students' safety is the main concern of the campus police, and they are ever-present.

Nevertheless, underage drinking is still pretty common, since minors are rarely caught. It is very easy for minors to buy drinks at bars. Apartment parties and frat parties also do not check IDs, so everyone can drink there. Most bars on campus do the opposite, and recently they have begun to crack down on fake IDs. Basically, if you have the money or the friends to do it, you can drink easily. Still, getting busted for being underage means taking a big risk. If you are caught, you might get a $200 drinking fine, jail time, or worse. As one student put it, it's just best to wait until you turn 21 and can go out to the bars and drink legally with your friends.

The College Prowler® Grade on

Campus Strictness: C+

A high Campus Strictness grade implies an overall lenient atmosphere; police and RAs are fairly tolerant, and the administration's rules are flexible.

Parking

The Lowdown On...
Parking

Approximate Parking Permit Cost:

$312 per year

U of I Parking Services:

Public Safety Building, MC-241

1110 W. Springfield Ave.,
Suite 201, Urbana

(217) 333-3530

comments2@oandm.uiuc.edu

www.parking.uiuc.edu

Common Parking Tickets:

Expired meter: $10

No-parking zone: $30

Fire lane: $100

Handicapped zone: $100

Student Parking Lot?

Yes

Freshmen Allowed to Park?

Yes

Parking Permits

Students can get a permit pretty easily. Unfortunately, only two lots are open for student use, F23 and E14, both of which are a good walk from campus and the dorms. To get a permit, all you have to do is call the office and reserve one. When you pick it up, you need your license plate number, registration, driver's license, and payment.

Did You Know?

Best Places to Find a Parking Spot

- Meters around the Quad (usually full, unless you come right before the hour, when students leave class)
- Meters off of Daniels or Third Street
- Apartment lots (but don't leave your car for too long, or you will get towed!)
- Meters after 5 p.m.

Good Luck Getting a Parking Spot Here:

- Urbana-Champaign . . . especially anything on or near Green Street.

Students Speak Out On...
Parking

"It's not recommended for students to bring cars on campus because of the high parking fees (around $200 per semester). Then there are traffic violations to worry about (and obnoxious parking meters)."

Q "Parking is a nightmare on campus. Because it is a large school, many people are driving, and there is **only a limited amount of parking spots**. If one has to drive to campus, he or she might have to leave pretty early to find or wait for a spot."

Q "I don't have a car, but I know **it is hard to find a place**, especially when going to class in the morning. You have to come back every two hours because of the meters, or you get a ticket."

Q "Having a car can be **more work for students**. But its advantages mean not having to wait for the bus while you're trying to go see a movie that you're running a little late for."

Q "**Parking is very hard to find**. They have meters by the classrooms and rented spots by the apartments and frat houses. It costs a quarter for 20 minutes, and they always come check at the 50-minute mark every hour when classes let out so you have to pay the whole 75 cents or you will get a ticket."

Q "**They will not hesitate to tow your car** here. There are three towing companies in the city and it can cost anywhere between $75 and $85 to retrieve your car. The car may be convenient, but you have to either pay for a space or rack up tickets, so it's going to cost you no matter what."

Q "The meter men are [expletive]. If you are just sitting five minutes in a spot, **they come over to you in their little shorts and demand that you pay up**. Man, get a real job already."

Q "Parking is an issue on campus. **Metered parking is available**, but is often taken and hard to rely on if you're trying to get to class on time."

Q "Parking passes are available for students living in dorms. They are **first come, first served**, so if you do not get one early, you may be assigned a spot in a remote lot where you can take the bus and be placed on a waiting list for a closer spot."

Q "I had a parking spot sophomore year in the student lot, and I am pretty sure that it wasn't even in the state. Oh well, at least **I lost weight walking to my car everyday**."

Q "There is a lot of parking. **Mostly meters**."

Q "Oh my gosh, **we have parking here**?"

Q "There are **two student lots on campus**. Yeah, just two. So good luck with that, kids."

Q "**A friend of mine was towed**. It was like five minutes to six, but she still got towed."

The College Prowler Take On...
Parking

Finding a parking spot on campus is pretty much impossible. If you have a yearning to drive to class—and when it is 19 degrees outside, who can blame you? You will find yourself circling the streets, chasing after anyone who looks like they might be leaving their parking spot. If you have to leave your car for more than a couple of hours, you might as well just take the bus or walk, unless you are rich and you want to spend $5 on parking a day. If you have just a quick errand or one class, allot yourself some searching time. Look out for the parking police who take their job very seriously. You would think they are on a mission to save the free world or something, with the zeal they have for their job.

If you are a student living in the dorms, you should pretty much give up on having your car with you. The student parking lots are blocks away from most of the dorms, although people who live in FAR/PAR are conveniently close to F23. If you are living in private housing or an apartment, finding a permanent space won't be a problem, although it may be costly. U of I really needs to build more student lots, and, someday, maybe they will use all the money they make from tickets to do so, but for right now, this campus is a parking nightmare.

The College Prowler® Grade on
Parking: D

A high grade in this section indicates that parking is both available and affordable, and that parking enforcement isn't overly severe.

Transportation

The Lowdown On...
Transportation

Ways to Get Around Town:

On Campus
Safe Rides, 9 p.m. to 6 a.m.,
(217) 265-7433

Student Patrol Walking Escorts
9 p.m.–2 a.m. Sunday–Thursday,
9 p.m.–3 a.m. Friday–Saturday
(217) 333-1216

Public Transportation
Champaign-Urbana Mass
Transit District, bus schedules
online at
www.cumtd.com/mtdinfo.html
(217) 384-8188

Taxi Cabs
C-U Taxi,
(217) 359-8634
Radio Cab Co,
(217) 355-1355
Illini Limo,
(217) 384-5892

Car Rentals

Alamo, local: (217) 352-2775;
national: (800) 327-9633,
www.alamo.com

Avis, local: (217) 359-5442;
national: (800) 831-2847,
www.avis.com

Budget, local: (217) 378-8584;
national: (800) 527-0700,
www.budget.com

Dollar, national:
(800) 800-4000.
www.dollar.com

Enterprise
local: (217) 351-1402;
national: (800) 736-8222,
www.enterprise.com

Hertz, local: (217) 359-5259;
national: (800) 654-3131,
www.hertz.com

National, local: (217) 359-5259;
national: (800) 227-7368,
www.nationalcar.com

Best Ways to Get Around Town

Walk

Campus MTD

Catch a ride with a friend

Ways to Get Out of Town:

Surburban Express
(217) 344-5500

Airlines Serving Urbana-Champaign

American Airlines,
(800) 433-7300
www.americanairlines.com

(Airlines, continued)

Continental, (800) 523-3273
www.continental.com

Delta, (800) 221-1212,
www.delta-air.com

Northwest, (800) 225-2525,
www.nwa.com

Southwest, (800) 435-9792,
www.southwest.com

TWA, (800) 221-2000,
www.twa.com

United, (800) 241-6522,
www.united.com

US Airways, (800) 428-4322,
www.usairways.com

Airport

Willard Airport
www.willardairport.com
(217) 244-8600

How to Get to the Airport

A cab or car service is your
best bet; a cab ride to the
airport costs $25.

The Greyhound service is in
downtown Champaign,
which is about two miles from
the center of campus. For
schedule information,
call (800) 231-2222.

Champaign Greyhound Terminal

45 E. University Avenue

Champaign, IL

(217) 352-4150

www.greyhound.com

Transportation

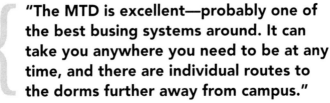

"The MTD is excellent—probably one of the best busing systems around. It can take you anywhere you need to be at any time, and there are individual routes to the dorms further away from campus."

Q "The bus system in C-U allows students **convenient and safe transportation**. The buses are coded using colors (excepting the '22 Illini bus), and provide schedules and route listings on board."

Q "Sometimes buses are pretty gross and just driving in them makes you smell. But **the MTD is always clean and comfortable**, albeit a little crowded at peak times."

Q "The buses work for me pretty well. **They go where I need them to** and I've never had a problem."

Q "If you don't have a car, getting to the movies takes 30 minutes instead of 10, when you take the bus. But **it gets you there**."

Q "**There is a great bus system**; you never have to worry about getting around and finding stuff."

Q "The MTD **gets you around campus pretty easily**."

Q "The buses are **free for University students to use**, and they even go as far as Parkland College, which is convenient for students who take classes at both schools. The grocery store and mall are also accessible by bus, as are bars and restaurants."

Q "**Public transportation is readily offered and encouraged**. Buses go everywhere, from the dorms to the different buildings and to off-campus areas like the mall. It was voted the best transit system in 1997 and 2001."

Q "**Public transportation is convenient** when you have nothing else to get around in. If you live at FAR, it is a way of life and can be journey trying to get from point A to point B."

Q "The buses seem great to me. I try not to make riding the bus seem too complicated though, because **the routes can really be confusing for an LAS major like myself**. I know how to get to class and home. Anything else is just showing off."

Q "During the winter months, **buses can run late and are very crowded**. Sometimes buses pass you up because the number of passengers outnumbers the seats/vacancy of spots."

Q "The buses get people home safely at night and get them to class on time in the morning; **it really is quite an impressive system**. The earlier you tackle it, the less likely that it will get the better of you."

Q "Every student has a bus pass and the buses run about five minutes apart. The #22 runs through the most central part of campus. It goes to the Union, the Six-Pack, both of the exercise facilities, and stops no more than a block away from every bar. **The buses run from 7 a.m. to 3 a.m.**"

The College Prowler Take On...
Transportation

Transportation around campus is pretty accessible. The MTD buses run all over campus, including downtown Urbana. They run regularly to the Quad and the main part of town, so you never have to wait for a ride. This is great if you are out late at night and are worried about returning to the dorms safely. As one student said, understand that the bus that will be coming in the next five minutes might not necessarily be the bus you need. However, if you are trying to make it to a distant location, you might have a wait, but usually no more than 15 or 20 minutes. Walking and biking are also good options, and if the weather is nice, most people don't mind burning off a few calories while going to class.

As for leaving town, the Suburban Express and Greyhound are great options. If you want to go home for a weekend or up to Chicago for a night or two, both are inexpensive and accessible means of transportation. Of course, it is nice to have your own car, or to at least to share a ride with friends, since this gives you more control and freedom. It is not a necessity, though, because the transportation around here is A-OK. But to make it better than A-OK, hop on the bus as early as possible in your college career and familiarize yourself with the routes and the schedules. If you wait until your senior year to finally figure out the bus system, you'll have missed out on one of the easiest transportation systems around.

A-

The College Prowler® Grade on
Transportation: A-

A high grade for Transportation indicates that campus buses, public buses, cabs, and rental cars are readily-available and affordable. Other determining factors include proximity to an airport and the necessity of transportation.

Weather

The Lowdown On...
Weather

Average Temperature:

Fall: 65°F
Winter: 30°F
Spring: 55°F
Summer: 73°F

Average Precipitation:

Fall: 3.22 in.
Winter: 2.01 in.
Spring: 4.80 in.
Summer: 4.21 in.

Students Speak Out On...
Weather

{ **"The weather fluctuates constantly. You need hot weather and cold weather clothes, 'cause it can change out of nowhere. All the seasons come into play on this campus."**

Q "You can never tell what the weather in Illinois will be like because **it constantly changes**. Bring whatever clothes seem comfortable and appropriate to you."

Q "The weather is **nice in the fall and late spring**. It is windy and stormy at times. The winters are pretty cold and snowy."

Q "The weather is nice. Some dorms have A/C. Go for the A/C. **Bring clothes you will feel comfortable in**."

Q "The weather sucks! Bring really warm clothing for the winter and a big umbrella. **It is so windy**!"

Q "In LAR, there is no air, so be prepared. At home, you are spoiled, always expecting air-conditioning to be on. Here, **you have to bring fans**. And in the winter, bundle up, because you have to walk in the cold."

Q "As a Midwestern school, UIUC has every type of weather. It will get hot in the summer, freezing in the winter, and everything in between. It is **a little windier than it is in Chicago and the suburbs**. Bring all types of clothes, because rain in June and snow in March is not impossible, however unlikely."

Q "**It is freezing cold to hot and sweltering**. Depending on when you go home, you can bring summer and fall clothing with you at the beginning of the year and get winter clothes later around fall break. Then, in the spring you can take home the winter clothes and bring back your spring/summer clothes at spring break."

Q "In actuality, **the weather in Champaign is hotter than that in Chicago**, and this causes a lot of students to pack light. People who are not from Chicago are often surprised and even dejected when the winter months roll around because it gets cold (but not as bad as Chicago)."

Q "**U of I is in the Midwest, and it gets pretty cold**. A lot of students come out from California and don't bring winter coats. Some of them have never seen snow. In mid February when winter is in full gear, not only will you be wearing a coat, scarf, gloves and hat, you will either get really intimate with the bus schedule, or you will pay for those parking meters."

Q "Summers in C-U get very hot, and winters get very cold. Be prepared for anything, because you will need it all. **The weather is often unpredictable**, and it can remain hot until November and cold until May."

Q "The weather really shocked me. **I was not prepared for it to be so cold** and wet in the winter. I was often going to class in sandals and a tank, only to find myself walking home in the snow!"

Q "You need every kind of clothing. And you should really try to get a dorm with A/C. And FYI, **the dorms start turning the heat on in October**, even though it could still be 60 degrees outside."

The College Prowler Take On...
Weather

The weather in Illinois has always been the butt of many jokes. Not only is it freezing cold one season and hellishly hot the next, but it is also completely unpredictable. You may leave the house in a sweatshirt and coat in February, only to find that it is 60 degrees outside. Or maybe you leave the house in April in a tank top, only to be surprised by a sudden snowfall. So basically, if you're not from the area or are not familiar with Midwest weather, you are definitely in for a few surprises.

The only thing you can do is be prepared. It is best to layer your clothing, especially if you have to walk anywhere. Students who dress like this always have clothing to bundle up in if it is cold, or they are always able to shed layers if it gets warm. It is definitely suggested that you bring an umbrella and snow gear, because Illinois is also home to a lot of snow and rain. Nothing sucks more than walking to class in three inches of snow and ice, but it is a reality that Illinois students have to face, so be warned. If you are not going to be able to make yourself go to class if it is below 32 degrees, then you might not want to go to school here. Maybe someday U of I will build underground tunnels for its students to walk to class in, but until that day, we will be stuck with dogsleds.

D

The College Prowler® Grade on

Weather: D

A high Weather grade designates that temperatures are mild and rarely reach extremes, that the campus tends to be sunny rather than rainy, and that weather is fairly consistent rather than unpredictable.

Report Card Summary

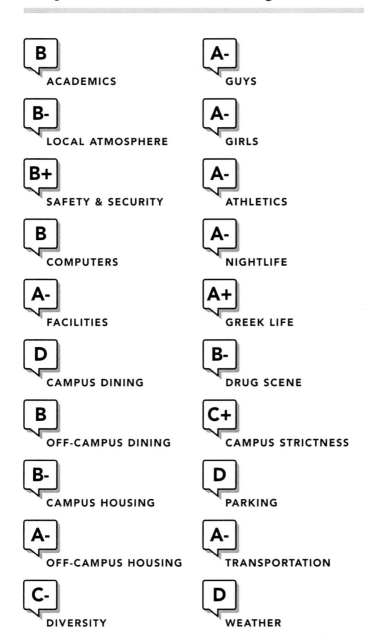

B
ACADEMICS

A-
GUYS

B-
LOCAL ATMOSPHERE

A-
GIRLS

B+
SAFETY & SECURITY

A-
ATHLETICS

B
COMPUTERS

A-
NIGHTLIFE

A-
FACILITIES

A+
GREEK LIFE

D
CAMPUS DINING

B-
DRUG SCENE

B
OFF-CAMPUS DINING

C+
CAMPUS STRICTNESS

B-
CAMPUS HOUSING

D
PARKING

A-
OFF-CAMPUS HOUSING

A-
TRANSPORTATION

C-
DIVERSITY

D
WEATHER

Overall Experience

Students Speak Out On...
Overall Experience

"There are pluses and minuses. What it offers is a quality education, a strong opportunity for activism, and a social scene that revolves around every individual's personal interests."

Q "When my mother exclaimed 'you made it—your first year,' I was so caught up in finals that I was so eager to leave. But ever since I returned home, **I have thought about school everyday**. The good times, the rough times, and how they were all worth it."

Q "At times, **I wish I was someplace warmer**, but this is a great school. It's been a truly unique experience for me. I am proud to be at a place that has such a rich tradition, not only athletically and socially, but academically as well."

Q "A diversity of people and ideas ensure that a person will not leave the same after four years. And though **it's frustrating to be in the middle of farmland**, there is not a moment of regret for choosing the University of Illinois."

Q "**I have had a very good undergraduate experience** at U of I, and I have realized that it is possible to have an enriching experience as long as you dedicate your time to getting involved in your schoolwork and in extracurricular organizations."

Q "I feel that **I am ready to move on in life**. Even though I will be spending more time at the University, I also know that the 'real world' will be a shock, and therefore am not regretting the time I have left too much."

Q "My overall experience at the University of Illinois has been great. **I cannot imagine being anywhere else**. It is big and to some it is overwhelming, but I love seeing everyone on the Quad and knowing we all have stresses and tests, but we make it through. A big part of it is finding a group or student organization to be involved in. Then, as you get to know people, the campus gets smaller and smaller, and you feel like you know a ton of people. It is really amazing to look back and realize how many people you have met over the years."

Q "The independence afforded by having an apartment and paying bills builds self-esteem and confidence, and **learning in the classroom builds academic and intellectual pride**. I have met many instructors that have become role models for me, and I found friends that have made my experience here even more rewarding."

Q "I hated it so much in the beginning. I just kept comparing it to my high school and whining to my parents. But then **I realized that I had to grow up**. And I am so honored that I got to do that at such a great school with so many great people."

Q "When I first came here, I admit that I all did was drink and blow off class. I really regret that, because I messed up not just my grades, but I also missed out on all the other opportunities there are here. Now that I am graduating, **I wished that I had used my time here better**."

Q "I am leaving here with friends from Turkey, China, Africa and, of course, Chicago. Where else can you do that, **where else can you meet that many people** and learn so many things?"

Q "When I was graduating high school, **I did not even want to go to college**. I just wanted to party and hang out in the small hometown I knew so well. The person I have become versus the person I used to be—only a great school could have effected that kind of change in me."

Q "Sometimes the tuition increases and bureaucratic stuff make me hate it here—but underneath it all, **I am glad to have this school right in my state**."

Q "**It has been a great experience here**. I've enjoyed a lot of new experiences and have met a lot of new people. I think I have made the right choice in coming here."

Q "It is easy to let the party scene get the best of you, but many students learn to take responsibility and create **a balance between school life and social life**."

Q "I have really loved it here. There are **great people and great teachers**—it is such a great school!"

Q "I have no doubt that **I will leave this school with a bright and limitless future** in front of me."

Q "My college experience is dear to me because **I have matured and changed so much** for the better."

Q "I have loved this experience. **No regrets whatsoever.**"

The College Prowler Take On...
Overall Experience

One might expect some tentative and even negative opinions about the school, but this is truly not the case here at U of I. Though students have had varied experiences here, both positive and negative; many say that they were and are glad to be students here. They are proud of U of I's history, proud of academic accomplishments, proud of the social opportunities, and, most of all, they are proud to be alumni. For so many students to view their time here as a positive experience, once all the pros and cons have been taken into consideration, is a fantastic testament to the University's strength.

Of course not everyone's school experience is enjoyable 100 percent of the time, and students here still had plenty to complain about—the weather, the parking, the Greek social scene, the rural location. But all things considered, the positive points of the U of I experience tipped the scale—the University's academic excellency, the safety, the social atmosphere, the athletic tradition, the city's excellent transportation system. Some students admitted that they had a hard time adjusting, that they occasionally wished they had made another decision—but in the end, they were all happy to be here. The most encouraging fact was that so many people mentioned that they were leaving as better people, more knowledgeable, eclectic, and better equipped to through navigate life. University of Illinois students do not just leave with a piece of paper in their hands, they leave with a wealth of experience and hope that is not easily rivaled.

The Inside Scoop

The Lowdown On...
The Inside Scoop

University of Illinois Slang:

Know the slang, know the school. The following is a list of things you really need to know before coming to U of I. The more of these words you know, the better off you'll be.

The Union – Main student center where everything happens, or at least everything legal.

The Quad – The name for the main area of campus, where the Union and major buildings are located.

The DI – The student-run campus newspaper.

The Six-Pack – Collection of six dorms that is known for its partying freshmen.

The Undergrad – The underground library for undergraduates.

Free Ride – Affectionate nickname for the SafeRides, since people basically use it as a free taxi cab.

Virgin Vault – What students call the all-girl dorms.

Alien Hall – The name for Allen Hall, home to musicians and artists.

→

GDI – Gosh-Darn Independents who won't go Greek, or something to that effect.

Unofficial Saint Patrick's Day – Biggest holiday of the year at U of I. Since students miss the real St. Patrick's Day because they are on spring break, they declare their own on March 8. Green beer starts flowing even before the rooster crows.

Banner – The name for the new online class registration system.

UI Direct – The old class registration system.

Timetable – Online or book course description with times.

Late Night Pizza – The legendary ISR pizza that you will dream about for years to come.

Wine Night – What people call Tuesdays at Clybourne.

Mathematica – An online system if you take a high level math or chemistry class.

Mallard – Online class notes and quizzes for foreign language classes.

Massmail – What you will get from the Chancellor every month, informing you and the rest of the campus about safety or world issues.

Free Absences – What you use when you sleep in or watch soaps instead of going to class. Usually a teacher gives out about 2–5 absences before docking your grade.

McKinley – The Health Center where you can go to get sick excuses for class, should your free absences run out.

The Stacks – Nickname for the bookshelves in the main library.

Preacher Dan – The scary guy on the Quad who tells us we are all going to Hell.

Things I Wish I Knew Before Coming to University of Illinois

- Don't live with someone you knew from high school. It never works out.

- Don't come to an un-air-conditioned dorm without a fan.

- Don't wear sandals or heels to walk to class. Even if they are cute.

- Buy lots of hoodies. Come November, you won't be wearing anything else.

- Don't come here expecting to eat in the dining halls. Store emergency "Pasta, again?" reserves in your room.

- Take advantage of the A La Carte meals. They might not be in your dorm cafeteria, but they are worth the trip.

- Learn the bus system the first week. Don't wait until your junior year to figure it out like I did.

- Skip the freshmen stuff if you can, especially the Assembly Hall gathering. You have had hot dogs before, thank you very much.

- Learn your social security number by heart. In a big school, it is practically your name.

- Always, always have your I-card with you. You need it to get on the bus, to eat, to get in your dorm, and to identify yourself at your exams.

Tips to Succeed at University of Illinois

- Don't get caught up in the drinking scene. You are here to learn. At least that's what they keep telling you.

- Don't drink in the middle of the week, unless it is vacation.

- Don't be mean to your teachers just because you think you pay them.

- Go to office hours.

- Go to class.

- Go to the library.

- Study in between classes. Don't just waste your time napping. It's better to work now, and then play later.

- Don't take an unfair grade lying down.

- Don't sleep with the professor for grades.

(Tips to Succeed, continued)

- Turn off your cell phone in class. Who are you, Paris Hilton?
- Familiarize yourself with the campus. You don't want to go walking around with a map the first two weeks.

University of Illinois Urban Legends

- Hugh Hefner supposedly donated all his *Playboy* issues to U of I.
- The English Building is haunted by the ghost of a girl who used to live there. So far, she has only made the power go out. But she is scheming. She is definitely scheming.
- The Assembly Hall was first designed by an architecture student. His teacher told him it was impossible and flunked him. Now it is one of the most admired buildings in the nation.

School Spirit

School spirit comes and goes in spurts. Everyone is very loyal during the first few weeks of the school year because they are all glad to be back and in good sprits. Then the winter wind starts blowing and none of us can figure out why we came to school here in the first place. When there is any work to be done, people are usually frustrated with being at college, but once the weekend starts, people don't really seem to mind. On the whole, though, everyone is usually happy with their college decision, and everyone always turns out to support the football team, no matter what the weather. If that isn't school spirit, then I don't know what is. Illini or bust.

Traditions

The Chief

The Chief was part of the U of I tradition for 70 years. He dressed in Native American garb and performed pseudo-Native American dances. Many activists felt that the Chief was racist towards Native Americans, since it used parts of their sacred culture for sport and laughs. The NCAA recently decided to mandate the elimination of the mascot, as well as similar mascots for several other universities.

Lincoln's Bust

Students with tests in Lincoln Theater often rub the nose on Lincoln's bust for luck. After decades of use, the glaze on the bust has been worn away, thanks to anxious test-takers.

"Illibuck"

The "Illibuck" was a turtle that was used as trophy between the Ohio Buckeyes and the Fighting Illini. After years of changing locations, "Illibuck" unfortunately passed on, and he has now been replaced by new turtles: Sachem of Illinois, and Bucket and Dipper of Ohio State. These turtles maintain peaceful relationships between the two warring teams.

Unofficial St. Patrick's Day

Unofficial St. Patrick's Day is celebrated on March 8 of the school year. Because students are generally gone on spring break during the real St. Patrick's Day, unofficial St. Patrick's Day was invented so that the students would not lose out on a perfectly good drinking holiday. Some students even go to class drunk on this day—not recommended.

Shoutouts

The student paper, the *Daily Illini*, used to run shoutouts every Thursday in its Buzz section. These shoutouts ranged from the funny to the romantic; the mean to the sentimental. They have recently been discontinued, but there is still a space for shoutouts to seniors in the graduation paper.

(Traditions, continued)

Outdoor Movie

A couple times a year, U of I hosts movies outside on the Quad. People gather on the grass with blankets and food and just hang out. It is one of the students' favorite traditions, and it's also free.

Moms & Dads Weekend

Moms and Dads Weekend are two weekends out of the year in which parents are encouraged to come out and visit their children. There are different events planned, ranging from football games to flower shows and fashion extravaganzas. It may be a little stereotypical, but it is still a tradition. It is a good time to visit with your parents and show them the campus, and it is doubly nice because you don't have to worry about what to do with them, since the whole thing has already been planned.

Finding a Job or Internship

The Lowdown On...
Finding a Job or Internship

The Career Center on Wright Street is essential. Even if you are uncertain about your major or goals, the people at the Career Center can give you tests and books to help you find out what you want to do. There is nothing wrong with being undecided, but eventually you are going to have to make some firm goals, and the Career Center is there to help you do just that.

Advice

Talk to professors that are teaching in your field. See what advice they can offer and what decisions they made. Also, almost every major has an information night, so pick a few that interest you and check them out.

Be sure to check out *www.pb.uillinois.edu*, the fantastically detailed University Office for Planning & Budgeting Web page reports. Click on "Custom Reports," "Department," "Urbana," and then select a department or concentration from the drop-down menu. From here, you can access detailed statistics about all reporting graduates' salaries, job satisfaction, and much more.

The Career Center also offers access to a number of local and international job search methods, all of which are available through *www.careercenter.uiuc.edu*.

Career Center Resources & Services

Career counseling

Career fairs and special events

Externships

Mock interview

Pre-health advising

Presentations

Resource center books, magazines, and eResources

Résumé and cover letter reviews

Workshops

Graduates Who Enter Job Market Within

Six Months: 67%

One Year: 82%

Two Years: 89%

Firms that Most Frequently Hire Graduates

Bank One, British Petroleum/Amoco, Caterpillar, Deloitte and Touche, Dupont, Exxon Mobile, Frito-Lay, General Electric, General Mills, Hormel Foods, Kimberly-Clark, Kraft Foods, Proctor & Gamble, Quaker Oats, Sears, Shell

Average Salary Information

The following statistics represent the mean beginning salaries for U of I graduates. They are separated based on department.

Accounting	$48,304
Aerospace Engineering	$42,765
Agriculture/Horticulture	$49,377
Animal Studies	$53,512
Anthropology	$42,186
Archaeology	$43,984
Architecture	$48,532
Architecture & Urban Planning Department	$69,386
Astronomy	$71,588
Athletics/Training	$45,777
Automotive Engineering	$28,359
Biology	$56,142
Business	$51,645
Chemical Engineering	$60,197
Chemistry	$47,659
Civil Engineering	$48,757
Communications	$40,134
Computer Engineering	$55,588
Computer Science	$53,151
Criminal	$47,375
Cultures/Civilization	$81,523
Design Arts - Industrial Design/ Graphic Design	$44,836
Economics	$61,988
Education	$37,089
Electrical Engineering	$56,218

Engineering Department	$50,891
English	$39,128
Finance	$83,479
Fine Arts - Painting/Sculpture/Photography	$56,256
and Geosciences	$59,738
History/Histories (art history/etc.)	$43,939
Industrial Design	$21,830
Industrial Operations Engineering	$51,648
Interior Design	$35,265
Journalism	$37,420
Kinesiology	$79,340
Language - French/Spanish/etc.	$37,637
Linguistics	$40,134
Math	$40,011
Mechanical Engineering	$57,317
Meteorology	$75,000
Music - Composition/Theory	$27,994
Music - Performance	$43,879
Music Education	$33,939
Natural Resources	$38,349
Naval Engineering	$50,000
Nuclear Engineering	$75,000
Nursing	$58,926
Other	$41,476
Perfomance Arts	$32,515
Pharmacy	$57,892
Philosophy	$59,288
Physical Therapy/Exercise Science	$31,504

Physics	$54,705
Political Science	$48,271
Dentistry	$47,076
Pre-law and Legal	$50,347
Pre-med and Medical	$66,283
Preparatory	$20,000
Pre-vet and Veterinary	$47,659
Psychology	$43,729
Public Health	$62,821
Public Policy	$44,602
Radiological Sciences	$50,000
Religion/Religious	$43,401
School of Information	$62,778
Social Work	$43,220
Sociology	$39,139
Telecommunications	$35,800
Undecided	$37,817
Urban Planning	$40,146
Video/Media	$26,703
Zoology	$20,000

Alumni

The Lowdown On...
Alumni

Web Site:
www.uiaa.org/urbana/index.html

Office:
Alumni Service Center
1401 W. Green Street,
Suite 227
Urbana, Il 61801
(800) 355-2586
alumni@uillinois.edu

Services Available:
Alumni Career Center
Credit Union
Explorers Travel Program
Find-A-Friend service
Library privileges
Loan consolidation
Online Directory
University of Illinois
MasterCard credit card

Major Alumni Events

Homecoming weekend and the Homecoming football games are the biggest events and they take place in late October. The Annual Reunion dinner hosted by the Illini Club in Chicago is also popular. It generally takes place in the summer and attracts majors and colleges of all types. Several alumni reunions and other events take place throughout the year, so check out the school calendar for information about specific class reunions and departments.

Alumni Publications

Illinois Alumni

This magazine comes out six times a year, and an annual membership is $30. You can also apply for the online printed version. It has news about old classmates and peers, and up-to-date information about University happenings.

Did You Know?

Famous UI Alums:

Dick Butkus (Class of '79) – football Hall of Famer

Michael Colgrass (Class of '56) – received the Pulitzer Prize in music for his piece 'Déjà Vu,' which premiered with the New York Philharmonic

Roger Ebert (Class of '64) – world-renowned film critic, first and only person to win a Pulitzer Prize for film commentary

Hugh Hefner (Class of '49) – *Playboy* creator

Andy Richter (Attended '84-'85) – Conan O'Brien sidekick and sitcom star

Wendell Stanley (Class of '27) – received the Nobel Prize in 1946 for research on virus proteins

Rosalyn Sussman Yallow (Class of '42) – invented radioimmunoassay, second woman to win the Nobel Prize in medicine

---

Student Organizations

There are nearly 1,000 student organizations at U of I; a brief sampling of these appears below. For a full listing and description, including contact info, go to *www.union.uiuc.edu/involvement/a-z_list.html.*

Apostolic Christian Youth Group
Baptist Student Foundation Campus Ministry
Black Chorus at the University of Illinois
Buddhism Study Group
Central and South American Student Association
Chinese Movie Club
Falun Dafa Practice Group
Fellowship of Catholic University Students
Fine Arts and Cultural Outreach Initiative
Intervarsity Christian Fellowship - Champaign Chapter
Lutheran Student Movement
Malaysian Students Association (MASA)
Mexican Student Association
Minority Organization for Artists
Open Doors Ministries
The Network Catholic Fellowship
Youth for Christ

The Best & Worst

The Ten **BEST** Things About University of Illinois

1. Meeting new people every day

2. Staying up 'til 4 a.m. eating Gumby's with friends

3. Just a short drive from home for most people

4. Having the biggest library in the nation and the best art museum and theater in the region

5. Taking a required class only to discover that you have found your career

6. Playing in the snow on the Quad

7. Buying books for $400 and then using them as coasters for the rest of the semester

8. Green Street has nothing but bars

9. Playing Frisbee or sunning on the Quad in the spring

10. Coming in as a clueless teenager, and leaving as a prepared adult

The Ten **WORST** Things About University of Illinois

1 Feeling like a number

2 The dining halls

3 No parking

4 Atmosphere lacks diversity

5 Required classes that are useless

6 Walking to class in the freezing cold and ice

7 Buying books for $400 and getting $30 back at the semester's end

8 Green Street has nothing but bars

9 Sweating on the way to class in the heat

10 Having to graduate and grow up

Visiting

The Lowdown On...
Visiting

Hotel Information:

Comfort Inn
305 W. Marketview Dr.
Champaign, IL
(217) 352-4055
Distance from Campus:
3.5 miles
Price Range: $77–$83

Courtyard by Marriott Champaign
1811 Moreland Blvd.
Champaign, IL
(217) 355-0411
Distance from campus: 3 miles
Price Range: $71–$84

Days Inn
1019 W. Bloomington Rd.
Champaign, IL
(217) 356-6973
Distance from Campus: 3 miles
Price Range: $50–$56

Drury Hotels

905 W. Anthony Dr.
Champaign, IL
(217) 390-0900
Distance from Campus: a little
over 3 miles
Price Range: $89–$95
*www.druryhotels.com/index.
cfm*

Econo Lodge and Suites

914 W Bloomington Rd.
Champaign, IL
(217) 356-6000
Distance from Campus: 3 miles
Price Range: $49–$59

Extended Stay Champaign-Urbana

610 W. Marketview Dr.
Champaign, IL
(217) 351-8899
Distance from Campus:
3.5 miles
Price Range: $55

Fairfield Inn

1807 Moreland Blvd.
Champaign, IL
(217) 355-0604
Distance from Campus: 3 miles
Price Range: $76–$80

The Hampton Inn at U of I

1200 W. University Campus
Urbana, IL
(217) 337-1100

(Hampton Inn, continued)

Distance from Campus:
About a mile
Price Range: $75–$89

Hawthorn Suites, Ltd.

101 Trade Centre Dr.
Champaign, IL
(217) 398-3400
Distance from Campus:
1.5 miles
Price Range: $70–$89

Holiday Inn

1001 Killarney St.
Urbana, IL
(217) 328-7900
Distance from Campus: 2 miles
Price Range: $69–$84

La Quinta Inn at Champaign

1900 Center Dr.
Champaign, IL
(217) 356-4000
Distance from Campus: 4 miles
Price Range: $62–$76

Microtel Inn

1615 Rion Dr.
Champaign, IL
(217) 398-4136
Distance from Campus: 6 miles
Price Range: $40–$50

Red Roof Inn Champaign
212 W. Anthony Dr.
Champaign, IL
(217) 352-0101
Distance from Campus:
2.7 miles
Price Range: $41–$51

Super 8 Champaign
202 W. Marketview Dr.
Champaign, IL
(217) 359-2388
Distance from Campus:
2.7 miles
Price Range: $43–$53

Campus Tours

The Campus Visitor Center is open Monday through Friday from 10 a.m. to 1 p.m. There are also select Saturday programs throughout the year, from September 12 to November 15. During this time, prospective students and visitors are given a tour and housing and admissions information. You must make a reservation. Call (217) 333-0824, or fill out the online form at *www.oar.uiuc.edu/prospective/visit/reserve.html*.

Take a Campus Virtual Tour

www.uiuc.edu/ricker/CampusTour

To Schedule a Group Information Session or Interview

Call the admissions office at (217) 333-0302 from 9 a.m. to 5 p.m. (central), or e-mail them at undergraduate@admissions.uiuc.edu.

Overnight Visits

Once you are accepted to U of I, you will be invited to an orientation weekend through the mail. If you choose to attend U of I, you can select a time you wish to visit the school during the summer. You will spend that time living in the dorms, eating in the dining halls, touring the Quad, and meeting with teachers and students in your field. This is also when you will register for the coming semester. Before you go, it might be a good idea to look at the courses online and plan your schedule ahead of time, since it will be your first time registering.

Directions to Campus

Driving from the North (Beginning at O'Hare Airport)

- Take I-90 to Interstate 194 for a few miles, to the Tri-State Tollway, Exit 1D.
- Head towards Indiana for 35 miles to I-80.
- Take I-80 West towards Iowa for a couple of miles.
- Exit off the left lane to I-57 South.
- Drive for approximately 2 hours until you reach I-74 in Champaign.
- Take I-74 East.
- In a few miles you should reach the Lincoln Avenue exit.
- Turn right and head to campus for about a mile.
- Driving from the South (Beginning at Lambert St. Louis Airport)
- Turn right on North Lindbergh/US-67.
- Go on the MO-B/Natural Bridge Road.
- Merge onto US-67.
- Quickly merge onto the exit for I-270.
- Remain on I-270 for about 30 miles, then merge onto I-70 east.
- Take I-70 to I-57.
- Take I-57 to I-74 East.
- After 3 miles, exit on the Lincoln Avenue exit.
- Turn right after the exit.

Driving from the East (Beginning at the Bloomington-Normal Airport)

- Take Route 9 West.
- Quickly merge left onto US-51/Veterans Parkway.
- After five miles, take US-51/Main Street Ramp.
- Keep left at the fork, turn left onto US-51/Main Street.
- Then take I-74 East towards Champaign.
- Exit off Lincoln Avenue.

Driving from the West (Beginning at Indianapolis International Airport)

- Drive east towards I-465.
- Travel north on I-465 to I-74.
- Take I-74 West at exit 16B.
- Travel for about 100 miles until you reach the campus.

Words to Know

Academic Probation – A suspension imposed on a student if he or she fails to keep up with the school's minimum academic requirements. Those unable to improve their grades after receiving this warning can face dismissal.

Beer Pong/Beirut – A drinking game involving cups of beer arranged in a pyramid shape on each side of a table. The goal is to get a ping pong ball into one of the opponent's cups by throwing the ball or hitting it with a paddle. If the ball lands in a cup, the opponent is required to drink the beer.

Bid – An invitation from a fraternity or sorority to 'pledge' (join) that specific house.

Blue-Light Phone – Brightly-colored phone posts with a blue light bulb on top. These phones exist for security purposes and are located at various outside locations around most campuses. In an emergency, a student can pick up one of these phones (free of charge) to connect with campus police or a security escort.

Campus Police – Police who are specifically assigned to a given institution. Campus police are typically not regular city officers; they are employed by the university in a full-time capacity.

Club Sports – A level of sports that falls somewhere between varsity and intramural. If a student is unable to commit to a varsity team but has a lot of passion for athletics, a club sport could be a better, less intense option. Even less demanding, intramural (IM) sports often involve no traveling and considerably less time.

Cocaine – An illegal drug. Also known as "coke" or "blow," cocaine often resembles a white crystalline or powdery substance. It is highly addictive and dangerous.

Common Application – An application with which students can apply to multiple schools.

Course Registration – The period of official class selection for the upcoming quarter or semester. Prior to registration, it is best to prepare several back-up courses in case a particular class becomes full. If a course is full, students can place themselves on the waitlist, although this still does not guarantee entry.

Division Athletics – Athletic classifications range from Division I to Division III. Division IA is the most competitive, while Division III is considered to be the least competitive.

Dorm – A dorm (or dormitory) is an on-campus housing facility. Dorms can provide a range of options from suite-style rooms to more communal options that include shared bathrooms. Most first-year students live in dorms. Some upperclassmen who wish to stay on campus also choose this option.

Early Action – An application option with which a student can apply to a school and receive an early acceptance response without a binding commitment. This system is becoming less and less available.

Early Decision – An application option that students should use only if they are certain they plan to attend the school in question. If a student applies using the early decision option and is admitted, he or she is required and bound to attend that university. Admission rates are usually higher among students who apply through early decision, as the student is clearly indicating that the school is his or her first choice.

Ecstasy – An illegal drug. Also known as "E" or "X," ecstasy looks like a pill and most resembles an aspirin. Considered a party drug, ecstasy is very dangerous and can be deadly.

Ethernet – An extremely fast Internet connection available in most university-owned residence halls. To use an Ethernet connection properly, a student will need a network card and cable for his or her computer.

Fake ID – A counterfeit identification card that contains false information. Most commonly, students get fake IDs with altered birthdates so that they appear to be older than 21 (and therefore of legal drinking age). Even though it is illegal, many college students have fake IDs in hopes of purchasing alcohol or getting into bars.

Frosh – Slang for "freshman" or "freshmen."

Hazing – Initiation rituals administered by some fraternities or sororities as part of the pledging process. Many universities have outlawed hazing due to its degrading, and sometimes dangerous, nature.

Intramurals (IMs) – A popular, and usually free, sport league in which students create teams and compete against one another. These sports vary in competitiveness and can include a range of activities—everything from billiards to water polo. IM sports are a great way to meet people with similar interests.

Keg – Officially called a half-barrel, a keg contains roughly 200 12-ounce servings of beer.

LSD – An illegal drug, also known as acid, this hallucinogenic drug most commonly resembles a tab of paper.

Marijuana – An illegal drug, also known as weed or pot; along with alcohol, marijuana is one of the most commonly-found drugs on campuses across the country.

Major –The focal point of a student's college studies; a specific topic that is studied for a degree. Examples of majors include physics, English, history, computer science, economics, business, and music. Many students decide on a specific major before arriving on campus, while others are simply "undecided" until declaring a major. Those who are extremely interested in two areas can also choose to double major.

Meal Block – The equivalent of one meal. Students on a meal plan usually receive a fixed number of meals per week. Each meal, or "block," can be redeemed at the school's dining facilities in place of cash. Often, a student's weekly allotment of meal blocks will be forfeited if not used.

Minor – An additional focal point in a student's education. Often serving as a complement or addition to a student's main area of focus, a minor has fewer requirements and prerequisites to fulfill than a major. Minors are not required for graduation from most schools; however some students who want to explore many different interests choose to pursue both a major and a minor.

Mushrooms – An illegal drug. Also known as "'shrooms," this drug resembles regular mushrooms but is extremely hallucinogenic.

Off-Campus Housing – Housing from a particular landlord or rental group that is not affiliated with the university. Depending on the college, off-campus housing can range from extremely popular to non-existent. Students who choose to live off campus are typically given more freedom, but they also have to deal with possible subletting scenarios, furniture, bills, and other issues. In addition to these factors, rental prices and distance often affect a student's decision to move off campus.

Office Hours – Time that teachers set aside for students who have questions about coursework. Office hours are a good forum for students to go over any problems and to show interest in the subject material.

Pledging – The early phase of joining a fraternity or sorority, pledging takes place after a student has gone through rush and received a bid. Pledging usually lasts between one and two semesters. Once the pledging period is complete and a particular student has done everything that is required to become a member, that student is considered a brother or sister. If a fraternity or a sorority would decide to "haze" a group of students, this initiation would take place during the pledging period.

Private Institution – A school that does not use tax revenue to subsidize education costs. Private schools typically cost more than public schools and are usually smaller.

Prof – Slang for "professor."

Public Institution – A school that uses tax revenue to subsidize education costs. Public schools are often a good value for in-state residents and tend to be larger than most private colleges.

Quarter System (or Trimester System) – A type of academic calendar system. In this setup, students take classes for three academic periods. The first quarter usually starts in late September or early October and concludes right before Christmas. The second quarter usually starts around early to mid–January and finishes up around March or April. The last academic quarter, or "third quarter," usually starts in late March or early April and finishes up in late May or Mid-June. The fourth quarter is summer. The major difference between the quarter system and semester system is that students take more, less comprehensive courses under the quarter calendar.

RA (Resident Assistant) – A student leader who is assigned to a particular floor in a dormitory in order to help to the other students who live there. An RA's duties include ensuring student safety and providing assistance wherever possible.

Recitation – An extension of a specific course; a review session. Some classes, particularly large lectures, are supplemented with mandatory recitation sessions that provide a relatively personal class setting.

Rolling Admissions – A form of admissions. Most commonly found at public institutions, schools with this type of policy continue to accept students throughout the year until their class sizes are met. For example, some schools begin accepting students as early as December and will continue to do so until April or May.

Room and Board – This figure is typically the combined cost of a university-owned room and a meal plan.

Room Draw/Housing Lottery – A common way to pick on-campus room assignments for the following year. If a student decides to remain in university-owned housing, he or she is assigned a unique number that, along with seniority, is used to determine his or her housing for the next year.

Rush – The period in which students can meet the brothers and sisters of a particular chapter and find out if a given fraternity or sorority is right for them. Rushing a fraternity or a sorority is not a requirement at any school. The goal of rush is to give students who are serious about pledging a feel for what to expect.

Semester System – The most common type of academic calendar system at college campuses. This setup typically includes two semesters in a given school year. The fall semester starts around the end of August or early September and concludes before winter vacation. The spring semester usually starts in mid-January and ends in late April or May.

Student Center/Rec Center/Student Union – A common area on campus that often contains study areas, recreation facilities, and eateries. This building is often a good place to meet up with fellow students; depending on the school, the student center can have a huge role or a non-existent role in campus life.

Student ID – A university-issued photo ID that serves as a student's key to school-related functions. Some schools require students to show these cards in order to get into dorms, libraries, cafeterias, and other facilities. In addition to storing meal plan information, in some cases, a student ID can actually work as a debit card and allow students to purchase things from bookstores or local shops.

Suite – A type of dorm room. Unlike dorms that feature communal bathrooms shared by the entire floor, suites offer bathrooms shared only among the suite. Suite-style dorm rooms can house anywhere from two to ten students.

TA (Teacher's Assistant) – An undergraduate or grad student who helps in some manner with a specific course. In some cases, a TA will teach a class, assist a professor, grade assignments, or conduct office hours.

Undergraduate – A student in the process of studying for his or her bachelor's degree.

ABOUT THE AUTHOR

Writing this book has taught me more about my school than living here for three years has. I cannot believe how much stuff I did not know. Hopefully, it has helped you make a more educated decision about your college choice; I only wish that I had utilized some of this information for myself a little earlier. As it is, I only have two semesters left before I graduate with a degree in English. After that, I hope to continue writing in some other form, whenever and wherever I can. I know that U of I is not the typical school one thinks of when it comes to art and literature, but I believe that it has truly helped me to become a better writer, and more importantly, a wiser observer. The teachers that I have had here have been absolutely dedicated to their students, willing and able to spend extra time with everyone. In the end, that is what has made U of I such a positive experience for me. At a big school like this, you really need teachers who will reach out to their students and build personal relationships with them, and that is exactly what we have here.

It is this proximity that first attracted me to the University of Illinois. While my sister chose to live 12 hours from home at an Eastern university, I knew I needed closer ties to my hometown and family, particularly since I was only 16 years old. While most people headed off to college are generally more mature than I was, being close to home and family is important for most people.

I would like to thank my writing manager, Joey Rahimi, for all the help he has given throughout this sometimes confusing experience. I would also like to thank all of my English teachers who have put up with my run-ons, my comma obsession, and my overuse of the word "consequently." Finally, I would like to thank my family for all of their help and patience. Thanks guys!

Bridget Sharkey
bridgetsharkey@collegeprowler.com

California Colleges

California dreamin'?
This book is a must have for you!

CALIFORNIA COLLEGES
7¼" X 10", 762 Pages Paperback
$29.95 Retail
1-59658-501-3

Stanford, UC Berkeley, Caltech—California is home to some of America's greatest institutes of higher learning. *California Colleges* gives the lowdown on 24 of the best, side by side, in one prodigious volume.

New England Colleges

Looking for peace in the Northeast?
Pick up this regional guide to New England!

NEW ENGLAND COLLEGES
7¼" X 10", 1015 Pages Paperback
$29.95 Retail
1-59658-504-8

New England is the birthplace of many prestigious universities, and with so many to choose from, picking the right school can be a tough decision. With inside information on over 34 competive Northeastern schools, *New England Colleges* provides the same high-quality information prospective students expect from College Prowler in one all-inclusive, easy-to-use reference.

Schools of the South

Headin' down south? This book will help you find your way to the perfect school!

SCHOOLS OF THE SOUTH
7¼" X 10", 773 Pages Paperback
$29.95 Retail
1-59658-503-X

Southern pride is always strong. Whether it's across town or across state, many Southern students are devoted to their home sweet home. *Schools of the South* offers an honest student perspective on 36 universities available south of the Mason-Dixon.

Untangling
the Ivy League

The ultimate book for everything Ivy!

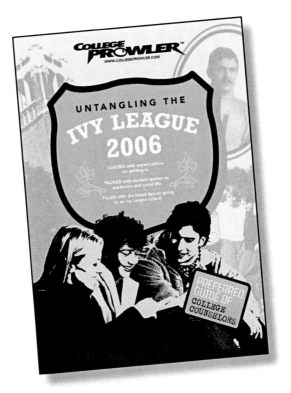

UNTANGLING THE IVY LEAGUE
7¼" X 10", 567 Pages Paperback
$24.95 Retail
1-59658-500-5

Ivy League students, alumni, admissions officers,
and other top insiders get together to tell it like it is.
Untangling the Ivy League covers every aspect—from
admissions and athletics to secret societies and urban
legends—of the nation's eight oldest, wealthiest, and
most competitive colleges and universities.

Need Help Paying For School?

Apply for our scholarship!

College Prowler awards thousands of dollars a year
to students who compose the best essays.
E-mail scholarship@collegeprowler.com for more
information, or call 1-800-290-2682.

Apply now at ***www.collegeprowler.com***

Tell Us What Life Is Really Like at Your School!

Have you ever wanted to let people know what your college is really like? Now's your chance to help millions of high school students choose the right college.

Let your voice be heard.

Check out ***www.collegeprowler.com*** for more info!

Need More Help?

Do you have more questions about this school? Can't find a certain statistic? College Prowler is here to help. We are the best source of college information out there. We have a network of thousands of students who can get the latest information on any school to you ASAP. E-mail us at info@collegeprowler.com with your college-related questions.

E-Mail Us Your College-Related Questions!

Check out *www.collegeprowler.com* for more details.
1-800-290-2682

Write For Us!

Get published! Voice your opinion.

Writing a College Prowler guidebook is both fun and rewarding; our open-ended format allows your own creativity free reign. Our writers have been featured in national newspapers and have seen their names in bookstores across the country. Now is your chance to break into the publishing industry with one of the country's fastest-growing publishers!

Apply now at **www.collegeprowler.com**

Contact editor@collegeprowler.com or call 1-800-290-2682 for more details.

Pros and Cons

Still can't figure out if this is the right school for you?
You've already read through this in-depth guide; why not
list the pros and cons? It will really help with narrowing down
your decision and determining whether or not
this school is right for you.

Pros	Cons
....	....
....	....
....	....
....	....
....	....
....	....
....	....
....	....
....	....
....	....
....	....
....	....
....	....

Pros and Cons

Still can't figure out if this is the right school for you?
You've already read through this in-depth guide; why not
list the pros and cons? It will really help with narrowing down
your decision and determining whether or not
this school is right for you.

Pros	Cons
....	....
....	....
....	....
....	....
....	....
....	....
....	....
....	....
....	....
....	....
....	....
....	....
....	....

Notes

....

....

....

....

....

....

....

....

....

....

....

....

....